CONSCIOUS
GLOBALISM

What's wrong with the world and how to fix it

David A. Schwerin, Ph.D.

Visit our Web site: *www.consciousthinking.com*

Cover and interior design by 1106 Design

First printing, June 2005
Printed in U.S.A. on recycled paper

Publisher's Cataloging-in-Publication
(Provided by Quality Books, Inc.)

    Schwerin, David A., 1942-
       Conscious globalism : what's wrong with the world and
    how to fix it / David A. Schwerin.
       p. cm.
       Includes bibliographical references and index.
       LCCN 2005900239
       ISBN 0-9765189-3-7

       1. Globalization—Economic aspects. 2. Globalization
    —Social aspects. 3. Globalization—Political aspects.
    I. Title.

JZ1318.S37 2005   303.48'2
                 QBI05-200020

Table of Contents

Acknowledgments

I am extremely grateful for the support I received from friends and family throughout the period this book was written. First and foremost, I thank my wife, Joan, for her selfless service and wise counsel throughout this endeavor. Whenever I needed assistance, from the mundane to the extraordinary, she was there. When Joan gets her report card from the observers on high I certainly hope she gets all the plaudits she deserves. My son, Eric, was a joy to raise, a pleasure to watch mature and a delight to journey with regardless of the activity or subject. I consult him regularly and his insights and knowledge on politics and international relations were indispensable in the development of this book.

Barbara Good and Geoffrey Thomas provided valuable comments and suggestions shortly after the first draft was completed. Their initial encouragement kept me going through the many drafts that followed. Carolyn Tilove has been instrumental in deepening my understanding of myself and the world around me. Her feedback on several aspects of the manuscript was both perceptive and encouraging.

Tom Hubbard's constructive responses to my request for feedback supplied the motivation I needed to complete the final drafts of the manuscript. For taking valuable time away from his busy schedule, I am most appreciative. Arnie Shapiro's thorough review, of what I thought was the final draft, was above and beyond the call of duty. Whenever there is a need for assistance, I know I can count on Arnie.

Zhihe Wang, who translated Conscious Capitalism into Chinese and wrote the forward for the Chinese edition, continues to be a great source of help with this second book. With his enthusiastic support, I have no doubt Conscious Globalism will also find a receptive audience in China. Bruce Topman gave me an honest appraisal and professional guidance whenever I asked; I am grateful for his friendship.

Diane Muenz and Donna Strauss have provided inspirational support throughout the period I have been writing. I am eternally thankful for the insights, prodding and encouragement that have come through them. For Sharon Balsama and all those who make the Pathwork material so accessible and comprehensible, I am forever indebted.

Introduction

...the only real thriving school of globalists in the world today—hedge fund managers.
THOMAS FRIEDMAN, THE LEXUS AND THE OLIVE TREE

What in the world is going on? Why do so many business and political leaders behave in such an ignorant, irresponsible, manner? I don't understand!

Do thoughts such as these reverberate in your mind? Have your friends or family expressed similar sentiments? To paraphrase the astute, often quoted observation, if today's headlines don't disturb you, you're not paying attention. Anxiety, irritation and frustration seem unavoidable when information circles the globe at warp speed and the boundaries that made us feel safe are no longer operative.

Many books have been written about the challenges faced as cultures collide and the pace of life quickens. The rapid integration of our global village has—for good or for ill—altered the lives of all of us, from the poorest to the most extravagantly rich. To be clear, *Conscious Globalism* is not really a book about globalization. It is a book that uses the globalization drama to explore today's tension-laden conflicts. The first task is to describe the counterproductive behaviors so prevalent in the global marketplace. The second is to analyze the erroneous beliefs that motivate such conduct. Until our distorted beliefs are made conscious and the consequences clearly seen, change is not possible.

Beliefs, first shaped in childhood, determine behavior. Family background, cultural conditioning and life experiences continue molding our belief system and harden our thinking. Being presumptuous enough to write a book offering universal solutions to seemingly intractable problems obligates me to provide information to the reader about my experiences and values.

My life experiences, at least since adulthood, have naturally revolved around my vocation and avocation. For over 30 years I earned a living in the investment field. My career began as a securities analyst for a large bank; after several years I was given the opportunity to manage several hundred million dollars in commingled funds (mutual funds for the trust customers of the bank). While that sounds like chicken feed today, it was a lot of money in the early 1970s. Working for a large institution had its limits so, after eight years, I struck off on my own to establish an investment-counseling firm where I could manage portfolios and set up and run a hedge fund (a pool of money that uses a variety of sophisticated investment strategies). Now you see why I was so enamored by Friedman's quote about hedge fund managers and display it prominently at the beginning of this introduction. Needless to say, I agree with him. I also salute him on his masterfully written best seller. In some ways *Conscious Globalism* begins where *The Lexus and the Olive Tree* left off. Besides analyzing issues that have surfaced more recently—Argentina's economic collapse, the Enron and WorldCom debacles, global warming, the spread of terrorism and AIDS—the book addresses topics that most current affairs writers consider only superficially, if at all. More about that shortly.

In addition to the mandatory emphasis on economic prognostications, hedge fund and other investment managers have to be knowledgeable about (or at least conversant with) everything from political and fashion trends to crop and weather patterns. There is really very little that happens in the world that doesn't affect some type of investment somewhere. The investment business can, of course, be a frustrating endeavor. In a bull market you are not needed; in a bear market you can't help. In other words, don't confuse brilliance with a rising market or stupidity with a declining one. It took me almost 30 years to understand the implications of this truth; finally in my mid-50s I saw the light and sold the bulk of my business so I could pursue more satisfying endeavors. My business career helped me learn a great deal about myself and the world in which we live. This, in turn, motivated me to devote more time and effort to writing and speaking about the need to reassess how we relate to one another. To date I have had one book, *Conscious Capitalism: Principles for Prosperity* (Butterworth-Heinemann 1998), and several articles published in a number of countries around the world.

Much of my time is now centered on my avocation of the last 30 years—cosmology, the study of the genesis and development of the universe. My interest extends to the philosophic side of cosmology as I search for answers to the perennial questions: Where did we come from? Where are we going? What is our purpose for being here? My experiences and understandings about the mysteries of life have advanced to the point where I can confidently proclaim that I know relatively little about this mind-boggling creation; this realization is humbling indeed.

While my work has forced me to keep abreast of what is happening around the globe, I must admit I am still a bit baffled by what takes place in the political arena. I am truly fascinated with politics and politicians, but I struggle to understand all the machinations that emanate from the world's makers and breakers. I guess I need to change my drinking habits and consume more of the libations favored by the typical politico. Fortunately, my son, Eric, is a professional student of the arcane field of politics. During our frequent discussions, he keeps me up to date and informed about this important piece of the globalization puzzle.

Since he is my window to this world, readers should know a little about his prejudices and presumptions. Eric spent the first eight years of his professional life working for the U.S. Government. Splitting his time between the White House, as Director of Business Liaison, and the Commerce Department, as Senior Policy Advisor for International Trade, he has become a real fount of knowledge on most global integration issues. While I readily concede a bias, I have little doubt that, having left the government, he will have an illustrious career in the private sector.

Having talked glowingly about my son, it would be imprudent of me not to sing the praises of my wife, Joan. She is an idealist who doesn't let me get sloppy with my mind or lazy with my body, things I might otherwise tend to do. We have worked remarkably well together in our investment advisory firm for over 20 years and she is the editor of all my works. We have traveled throughout the world visiting over two-dozen countries and some of our unique travel experiences are documented in the chapters that follow. My journey would have been inconceivably difficult were it not for her selfless support and wise counsel.

With my personal background out of the way, a brief introduction to the book is in order.

Conscious Globalism undertakes to discover and examine the source of today's global conflicts, raise awareness of the part we play in creating our problems and provide a roadmap for changing behavior one challenging but rewarding step at a time. The book is divided into four parts. **The Scene** is a broad-brush summary of the globalization process and provides some essential background material for subsequent chapters. Today's most pressing issues are discussed in detail and the groundwork is laid for discovering pragmatic solutions based on an understanding of what really serves our best interest. **The Challenges** takes an in-depth look at the protagonists in this unfolding melodrama: political officials and their often unfathomable policies, the phobias and idiosyncrasies of too many self-serving business executives, environmentalists with their strong willed ideologies and nation states with their historical baggage and freshly brewed challenges. **The Flaws and Consequences** discusses the ramifications, intended and otherwise, of thinking and behaving as we always have. Ideas for turning things around—for creating opportunities to thrive and find meaning and fulfillment—are freely offered. A series of thought provoking self-assessment questions provides readers with tools to discover what motivates their behavior and, by implication, that of others. **The Possibilities** considers several transformational views on how we can best interact with one another. Examples of companies, communities and countries that have prospered by following a broader, more inclusive concept of self-interest are presented to show alternative paths to a more harmonious and rewarding world order.

The last few pages of Friedman's book raise the question as to how God fits into the all-too-frequent chaos we witness daily. He states, "I have been asked that question [about God] so many times while speaking to groups about this book." He then goes on to conclude, "One could write a book about these themes alone [God, spiritual meaning and values as they relate to globalization]." While there is no explicit mention of God in the chapters that follow, we need to be cognizant of the higher dimensions as we go about our daily chores. If we avoid this unseen reality in our lives we risk living in a meaningless world where we simply move from one crisis to another. Given the September 11, 2001 wakeup call, we must and can do better. It is my hope that *Conscious Globalism* presents a constructive framework for participating fully in the evolutionary subplot that is globalization.

PART ONE

THE SCENE

"The financial and technological innovations that bring us together in a 'global community' must be accompanied by a change in consciousness—an embrace of our human obligations. Indeed, pushing for positive change is a duty we all share."

DR. OSCAR ARIAS SANCHEZ
NOBEL PRIZE LAUREATE
FORMER PRESIDENT OF COSTA RICA

Chapter One

The What, Why, Who and Where of Globalization

What on Earth Is Going on?

Globalization is a word that evokes great passion—both in those who favor and those who oppose the process. In its broadest sense, globalization can be viewed as the world-wide integration of economic, political and social activities, and information. Capitalism—the economic system based on free markets and private ownership of property—is a vital facilitator of this process. Deregulating and privatizing make the economy of a country more competitive and, therefore, more attractive to both domestic and foreign investors. Many people complain about globalization; the shrillest outcry coming from those who believe the spread of capitalism exacerbates an already untenable disparity in the distribution of wealth. Critics, however, have been unable to articulate an alternative economic system that raises living standards as quickly or as effectively.

There are, of course, a variety of ways capitalism is practiced. The degree to which markets are free (i.e., unconstrained by laws and regulations) and the extent to which property is privately rather than state owned or controlled, differ considerably from country to country. The form of capitalism practiced in the United States is significantly different from that practiced in France, Sweden, Japan or Argentina. And each of these five countries has a much different capitalistic model from the one emerging in China. Differences in political, economic and cultural traditions effect how capitalism evolves within a country or region.

Economic globalization is a dynamic process that has been unfolding over many years. As Alan Greenspan, longtime Chairman of the Board of Governors of the U.S. Federal Reserve System, has stated, "...economic globalization was the 21st century version of debates over societal organization that go back at least to the dawn of the Industrial Revolution, and many of the intellectual roots of these debates go back far longer." In fact, the process can arguably be traced to the time our ancestors shifted their focus from an exclusive concern for their personal welfare to a more inclusive interest in the well-being of their friends and family. From this has come a progression that has widened humanity's attention. After some time, families joined together in tribes for the sake of personal security and economic efficiency. Before long, surrounding tribes joined together to form larger, more self-sufficient villages. Over time, cities and states were created for the sake of further effectiveness and safety. Eventually, larger socioeconomic groups united along regional lines; for instance, those living in coastal areas would become economically aligned while those living in interior regions would join together to promote their particular needs and interests. These alliances usually led to the formation of politically integrated states and countries. More recently, nations have developed confederations with other contiguous countries to form political and economic blocs providing benefits of scale and security; the European Union is a recent example of this type of amalgamation. The realization, over the last few decades, that all boundaries are inherently artificial and inefficient has provided the impetus for the creation of our current global community.

Chinese Connections

Before economic integration can be perfected, the citizens of the world must learn to live together in peace and harmony. While day-to-day news reports do not paint an encouraging picture, significant changes are taking place beneath the surface. This was never so clear to me as when my wife and I made a trip to China in September 2001. Within the first half of the 23-day lecture tour, I became acutely aware of how incredibly close and connected our world has become.

The trip had been set up to promote my book, *Conscious Capitalism: Principles of Prosperity*, which had just been translated into Chinese and published throughout the People's Republic of China. I gave nine presentations to groups of business executives, political leaders and a variety of university students and faculty. After each lecture there was a question and answer session followed by informal conversations with whoever was interested. My first surprise came when the audience, knowing I was a professional investment advisor, queried me about the United States stock market. I was startled by how much they knew about the workings of the market and astonished that so many people knew the precise level of both the Dow Jones and Nasdaq stock averages. On any given day, I'd be lucky to get within a couple dozen points of the closing levels of these popular indices. As I was soon to learn, stock market news and commentary is generally available and widely followed in the print and broadcast media throughout China.

My second surprise came shortly after a student by the name of Sunny (an English derivation of his Chinese name) approached me after a lecture in the city of Xian and asked my wife to take a picture of the two of us. Sunny and I started a wide-ranging conversation during which he asked me where I lived. "In the Philadelphia suburbs," I replied. His face lit up and he immediately began to tell me all about the Philadelphia 76ers (Philadelphia's professional basketball team) and their star player, Allen Iverson. Sunny was on his university's basketball team and was modeling his game after Iverson's. His knowledge of the 76ers exceeded much of what I, an avid fan, knew. Television—Sunny's window on international sports—has brought the world together in ways that would have been unimaginable only a few short years ago.

Shortly after my return to the United States, Sunny and I began an e-mail correspondence, discussing everything from the world of sports to ancient philosophers. He was in his last year of college and finding a job was at the top of his priority list. In one of his e-mails he asked for my advice about looking for employment. After getting some preliminary information about his interests and preferred work location, I told him that I had spent some time with the Senior Manager of Human Resources at Motorola Corporation's Beijing headquarters. In fact, I had spent a full day visiting the company, both at its headquarters and one of its main production facilities in Tianjin, just prior to finishing my China tour. I offered to e-mail my contact and see if I could assist him in any way. He was, of course, extremely grateful. Within hours of sending my e-mail I got a very cordial reply from the manager at Motorola who, while making no promises, encouraged Sunny to submit his resume so the company could learn more about his qualifications and interests. Presto—in the space of a few hours, I had become an international headhunter without ever leaving the comfort of my home office.

These three experiences vividly portray the growing connection of citizens everywhere. Making use of today's sophisticated telephony, television and computers, people can track their favorite sporting events, keep tabs on the ups and downs of stock markets on six continents and nurture far-flung business relationships before getting dressed.

Why Now?

The trend toward economic integration has been evident for a long time, but the move to a truly global economy has been a relatively recent phenomenon. In the 1980s, two developments had a particularly salutary effect on the integration process. The fall of the Berlin Wall was of immense importance in several ways. During the Cold War it was virtually impossible to go anywhere without being thwarted by some trade protection measures or financial controls. Diametrically opposed political and economic systems were interspersed throughout the world. On one side were the Communist and Socialist style economies that were, by and large, centrally planned. On the other, a wide variety of capitalistic systems varying from strong free-market orientation to those that were much closer to welfare states. Multilateral security and trade pacts created a patchwork of alliances that spread across all regions and crisscrossed most continents. Political and cultural differences were celebrated and nearly impenetrable walls and boundaries were proudly erected to control the movement of trade and finely filter the flow of most information.

When the Berlin Wall collapsed, two momentous changes took place. First, capitalism began supplanting all other economic systems. Second, productive capacity, which had been largely untapped or inefficiently utilized in the rigidly controlled planned economies, became available for more creative purposes. Thus the productive capacity of the world increased significantly and led to an ultra-competitive market for most goods and services. This latter development reduced or eliminated the ability of businesses to raise prices on all but the most unique products. Thus, maintaining the profitability of an enterprise increasingly depends on continual innovation and rigorous cost reductions.

The second crucial development propelling economic globalization is the widespread availability and pervasive use of the Internet. Initially designed as a secure way to convey military intelligence, the Internet has, over the last decade, evolved into a vast global system composed of networks of all sizes communicating almost instantaneously with one another.

While the Internet has become the consummate people-unifier, the desire to connect with our fellow human beings started long ago. Indeed, there are some clear parallels between the longing of people to communicate with one another and their tendency to gather together in increasingly larger groups. People began to expand the distance over which they could communicate when they started using drums and smoke signals to contact those in the surrounding areas. Considerably later, in 490 BC, Athenians sent runners to Marathon to announce their victory over the Persians; hence the use of the word marathon to describe a race of exactly that distance. In the 12th century, carrier pigeons were used to carry important messages, particularly in times of war; they remained in use until World War I. The Pony Express was probably the last of the non-mechanical methods used for communicating over significant distances.[1] In the mid-1800s technology provided a quantum leap in communication power with the invention of the telegraph.

Telegraph lines finally stretched from the East coast of the United States to the West coast in 1861. In 1886, Thomas Edison patented a device that combined a transmitter with a microphone. Several decades later, Edison's telephone had supplanted the telegraph as the primary means of long-distance communication. The first half of the twentieth century saw the radio and then television become the primary way people learned about the world in which they live. In 1951, UNIVAC (Universal Automatic Computer) became the first commercial electronic computer. Fast-forward to the 1990s and processing power so fast that, when linked to electronic networks, the computer is transformed into a highly versatile communications device. Today, computers can be connected to printers, scanners, modems, faxes and a growing number of wireless devices to communicate with anyone, anywhere, anytime.

While each of these communication enhancements has had a tremendous impact on our ability to interact, nothing has been as momentous as the rise of the Internet. It has reshaped the way products are classified, purchased and serviced. It has left an indelible mark on the way we work and play. And it has created a plethora of smarter, cheaper devices for accessing information of all forms and from all places. Thus the Internet—the crowning achievement of the Information Revolution—made pivotal changes in the way businesses and consumers interact and transact. First, almost everyone has simple, inexpensive access to practically unlimited information about most products and services. This creates conditions where the cost to start a new business and the cost to do comparison-shopping drop significantly, in many cases approaching zero. This dramatically boosts competition and tremendously speeds the pace at which products go from being a novelty to a commodity. As Thomas Friedman states,

In the walled-up Cold War system this process of going from innovation to commoditization happened at 10 miles per hour, because the barriers to entry into businesses were generally much higher and the barriers countries could erect around their economies were also much higher. In the globalization world, with the barriers now lowered or removed, this process is happening at 110 miles per hour.[2]

Furthermore, the Internet brings companies closer to their customers; consumers have an enhanced ability to reflect their specific desires back to businesses. If the business is not responsive, the consumer can quickly decide to patronize those companies willing to offer something better. Prior to the Internet, most companies could maintain high profit margins because the consumer lacked the ability to determine which competitors had superior offers. Now citizens around the globe can stay informed about the price and quality of products offered by vendors across the street or across the ocean.[3]

With the elimination of many political barriers and the abundance of information, global commerce has taken off. The Internet offers advantages to buyer and seller alike. Many would contend that the consumer has been the prime beneficiary and the driving force behind this explosive growth. For an example of the benefits derived from using the Internet, come along with me as I go car shopping.

Riding the Net

Buying a new car is a challenging chore—dreaded by some, savored by others. Choosing between the myriad makes and models is the first task. Then comes the part people either love or hate; haggling over price to minimize the amount of money left on the car dealer's negotiating table.

Strange though it may seem, I actually enjoy this part of the game. This despite the fact that, for the 30 plus years that I have been buying cars, the playing field has been stacked against me. Generally ignorant of the dealer's cost or manufacturer's incentives, I was forced to guess at the lowest price the sales manager would accept to consummate a sale. The maturing of the Internet has leveled the playing field and, for better or worse, taken a great deal of the challenge out of buying a car. Now people around the world have access to everything they ever wanted to know about automobiles. Whether the car was manufactured in Asia, Europe or the United States, the Internet provides facts and opinions galore on the automotive industry. In fact, all this information makes auto buying as close as possible to a perfectly competitive market. You can compare body styles, safety features, length, width, height and weight dimensions, creature comforts, ride characteristics, warranty protection—there is even an independently produced video of the car of your choice. Recommendations from experts and critiques by owners are widely available. The manufacturer's suggested retail price, the dealer's invoice price, plus details on promotional advances, advertising allowances and dealer holdbacks are all there for the taking. So also is the trade-in value of your current car—rated by its condition and geographic location. And if you really want to make life easy, you can contact a buying service through the net and allow a professional to do the negotiating for you.

In my case, the saleswoman giving me a test drive was initially very coy about how much of a discount from the sticker price I could reasonably expect. To get her to be more forthcoming, I casually told her that I knew all the pertinent information was available on the Internet. "Well," she groused, "you've been looking at the Internet!" "Is there a law against this?" I queried. Her attitude quickly changed once the Internet entered the equation. She said that the markup on the car was about 10 percent over the invoice price. What she initially withheld was the fact that anyone logging onto the auto dealer's home page could buy the car from a specifically assigned salesperson for a few hundred dollars over the dealer's cost. After I revealed my new information, she immediately let me know that she would also be allowed to sell me the car for the same low price. The Internet, playing-field-leveler par excellence, comes to the rescue. Buyer and seller are finally working from the same page and retailers have finally lost their ability to take advantage of consumer ignorance.

Automobiles, of course, are just one of an enormous number of products and services that can be purchased on the net. Products today are manufactured anywhere and sold everywhere—a global marketplace if ever there was one. As should be obvious, there is one downside to the Internet phenomenon; in order to hone my haggling skills, I must now resort to practicing on my wife.

Who Makes the Rules?

To paraphrase a well-known but distorted version of the golden rule: those who have the gold make the rules. In today's global economy the rule makers are those who have accumulated wealth or the financial institutions to which it has been entrusted. These institutions are the primary sources of capital in today's fast paced economy; corporations, particularly those that do business internationally are the second. These enterprises have been referred to as Multinational Corporations (MNCs) or, more recently, Transnational. While a technical distinction can be made, this work uses the terms interchangeably. Together they have become the movers and shakers to whom societies across the political spectrum, from the least potent to the most power-ful, pay homage.

MNCs are enterprises that own or manage facilities out-side the country in which they are headquartered; many are more economically powerful than the nations within whose borders they operate. While their overriding objective is to maximize the return on their investment, they have made significant contributions—sometimes deliberately, at other times unintentionally—to the cross-border exchange of ideas and innovations. A more detailed discussion of the influence of MNCs on the global economy will be found in the chap-ters that follow. This section will focus primarily on the impact financial intermediaries are making on nation states of all sizes and levels of development.

Financiers to the Rescue

Government policymakers around the world are predis-posed to fine-tune economic growth through fiscal and mon-etary policy. By expanding or contracting a nation's budget and money supply, politicians attempt to keep the economy growing steadily by providing sufficient liquidity to finance economic development. With little to constrain policymakers, there has been a tendency to err on the side of more rather than less stimulus. Seasoned politicians are continually reminded of the electorate's foremost priority—jobs, jobs, jobs. Using fiscal policy as their primary tool, politicians have no compunction against budget deficits to insure a growing econ-omy and a favorable climate for the re-election of incumbents. This indiscriminant priming of the fiscal pump played a sig-nificant, although by no means exclusive, part in the extraor-dinary rise in inflation between the 1960s and 1980s. As an example, inflation in the United States had been running at or below two percent for the first half of the 1960s. By the early

1980s, inflation had skyrocketed to 15 percent. With the pur-
chasing power of bondholder's interest and principal payments decimated, many on Wall Street began referring to
bonds as "certificates of confiscation." Double-digit interest
rates made the cost of money prohibitive; new investment was
thwarted and bond and stock markets around the world were
devastated. Finally, investors had endured enough. Money
managers of all types and descriptions—I call them Investor
Vigilantes or IVs—decided to take matters into their own
hands and furnish the discipline that politicians lacked. IVs
were just what the doctor ordered—no pun intended. Merrill
Lynch published an economic commentary in 1983, a short
time after inflation had peaked, that noted the changed
dynamics. In a matter-of-fact manner, they commented on the
new political reality and its likely consequences.

> *The financial and foreign exchange markets play an*
> *important role in our projection of secular disinflation.*
> *We believe that these markets have become more prone*
> *to react to an expansionary monetary and fiscal policy*
> *by increasing the inflation or cynicism premium built*
> *into interest rates. This should diminish the inflation-*
> *ary impact of such actions, but at the cost of slower*
> *growth. More importantly, it should dissuade policy*
> *makers from pursuing such policies.*[4]

With the investment community shunning securities that
did not provide adequate compensation for the inflationary
bias of the economy, the real level of interest rates (the nom-
inal rate less the inflation rate) was ratcheting higher.
Politicians knew that higher interest rates would adversely
affect most citizens—consumers with mortgages, credit
cards or auto loans and businesses that required external
financing to develop new products and expand operations.

They also realized that high interest rates dampen economic growth and hinder any attempt to revive a sluggish economy. None of this is acceptable to a politician seeking the support of the electorate.

In 1993, president-elect Bill Clinton met with his economic advisors to chart an economic recovery plan in the face of growing budget deficits. In an elaborate presentation, Clinton was shown how reduced government spending would reduce the deficit and—if bond investors were convinced that lower deficits were an integral part of a long-term strategy— decrease long-term interest rates as well. The advisors stressed that any deficit reduction plan must be credible to the financial community. Clinton responded, "You mean to tell me that the success of the program and my reelection hinges on the Federal Reserve and a bunch of [expletive deleted] bond traders?"[5] The economic team unanimously agreed. Clinton, along with politicians around the world, was beginning to recognize the escalating influence of the IVs.

Beginning in the early 1990s, another momentous event further usurped the power of the politicians. As alluded to earlier, the fall of the Berlin Wall and the worldwide proliferation of capitalism have expanded international trade on an unprecedented scale. Problems in one part of the world now affect all parts of the world and the ability of politicians to isolate and control their domestic economies has been dramatically reduced. Now that economic activity was no longer confined to national borders, the fiscal and monetary policies of individual countries began to have a diminished impact on the domestic economy. In addition, with world trade expanding and stock and bond markets established around the globe, investors can move their capital from place to place at a moment's notice. Every government is subject to an IV veto whenever the political or business environment becomes more inviting elsewhere.

The rise of the Investor Vigilantes and the fall of the "Wall" moved economic power from political potentates to fleet-footed financiers. The private sector replaced the public sector as the primary source of the investment capital needed to jump-start and sustain economic development. The IVs set the rules—a country that chooses to ignore those rules will pay a steep price in the form of a stagnant economy. As a result, investors are now courted from Eastern Europe to South America and everywhere in between.

Who Pays this Czech?

The fact that IVs were becoming essential to societies at all levels of development became crystal clear when my wife and I visited our son, Eric, in Czechoslovakia (now the Czech Republic). Upon graduating college, Eric decided he would take a year off and teach English abroad. While I admired his adventuresome spirit, I had some sleepless nights prior to his departure. I knew little about Czechoslovakia other than it had recently gained independence from the Soviet Union and had been an industrial powerhouse prior to World War II. I had also read that, with the Soviet occupation, fully 97 percent of Czech production was under state control. I had the image of a chaotic wasteland with little to recommend it for a visit let alone a long-term stay.

Undaunted, Eric left for Czechoslovakia in the summer of 1991 and took up residence in Moravska Trebova, a small city about a hundred miles southeast of Prague. This is where he had been assigned to teach both secondary school students and working adults. In November of that year, my wife and I decided to visit our son and see first hand how he was doing. Our flight touched down in Prague and, almost immediately, we were dazzled by its enchanting old world charm and sophistication. After two days of spectacular sightseeing, we set our sights on Moravska Trebova. The trip got off to an inauspicious start when the only car available for rental was a Czech-made Skoda, a stripped-down version of the Volkswagen Rabbit with little more than a gearshift, steering wheel and four tires. In addition, maps of the area were far from AAA quality and, as luck would have it, a light snow had begun to cover the ground. Fortunately, someone was watching over us as we traveled the hilly countryside without incident.

It turned out that Moravska Trebova was surprisingly picturesque and Eric, given his amicable nature, had made many friends. Other than a few stares from time to time, we were treated like royalty wherever we went. Arrangements had been made to house us in the large Soviet-built apartment complex where Eric lived; our flat (quite a bit larger than his) was simply adorned but quite functional. Over our several-day visit we were shown every nook and cranny of the town. Mary, one of Eric's adult students, invited us to a delicious dinner at her home. She appeared to be in her 60s and was obviously very fond of Eric. We quickly thought of her as his surrogate grandmother and were relieved to know she was watching out for him. Another day we were taken to lunch at the workers' cafeteria where a full course meal—the quantity far surpassing the quality—was served in non-descript surroundings; for 8¢ (Eric paid less) who could complain?

The day before we were set to leave, we got an official invitation to have lunch with the mayor at the poshest restaurant in town. We were shocked that the mayor even knew we were visiting let alone worthy of special attention. While we readily accepted, we wondered whether there was a specific purpose behind the invitation or if it was simply a case of Czech hospitality. About a dozen citizens greeted us as we entered the modestly decorated private room. The mayor was a handsome, congenial chap who, we soon found out, had his pulse on world events and their likely ramifications.

After some toasts and small talk it quickly became apparent why we had been invited. The conversation turned to a topic that was high on the mayor's agenda. He began to describe his ambitious plans to make Moravska Trebova a vacation Mecca for citizens in the surrounding area as well as for visitors from far and wide. He proudly pulled out a detailed architectural rendering of his plans to transform this quaint town into a thriving tourist attraction. All that was lacking was the funding for his project. He had heard that we were investment advisors and like any enterprising entrepreneur, he couldn't let us leave town without making his best sales pitch. I didn't have the heart to tell him that neither venture capital nor real estate lending was our area of expertise. So we listened politely and said we would let him know if we found anyone who might be interested in funding the project. The mayor had the right church but the wrong pew; the right profession but the wrong specialty. We did send a contribution to the library in the Gymnasium where Eric taught as a token of our appreciation for the considerate way he was treated. The money was enough to buy quite a few books but it would have barely covered the cost of laying a cornerstone for the new town square that the Mayor envisioned.

Sometime later I began to realize the vast sums of money that would be required to rejuvenate the former Soviet empire. With state subsidies quickly disappearing throughout Eastern Europe and most businesses unable to compete with Western management and technology, the new world order would force government officials to look to a variety of new and unconventional funding sources to reconstruct their economies. Investment capital was essential to rebuild decaying infrastructure and jump-start new enterprises. Competition to entice financial intermediaries to loosen their purse strings would be fierce and IVs could expect to be wined and dined. Using their new celebrity status, IVs and

MNCs began to have considerable influence over how a society determines its priorities and structures its institutions.

Terms of Engagement

Adam Smith, in the *Wealth of Nations*, emphasized the importance of a legal infrastructure to the proper functioning of a market economy:

> *Commerce and manufacturers can seldom flourish long in any state which does not enjoy a regular administration of justice, in which the people do not feel themselves secure in the possession of their property, in which the faith of contracts is not supported by law, and in which the authority of the state is not supposed to be regularly employed in enforcing the payments of debts from all those who are able to pay.*[6]

Following the advice of this most revered of economists, Investor Vigilantes and Multinational Corporations make the implementation of an enforceable legal system priority number one. Since they can pick and choose which countries they want to favor with their funds—a prerequisite for economic growth—they have significant influence over how a country formulates many of its laws and regulations. The laws the golden rule makers favor can generally be divided into two groups. The first group consists of policies and regulations that encourage certain societal values, structures or actions. First and foremost on their wish list is the institutionalizing of a market-based economy with little, if any, state ownership or control. An integral part of sustaining such a system is a free press and the requirement that all pertinent economic information be fully disclosed by the appropriate parties. A strong, fully convertible currency and the facilitation of direct foreign investments are other prerequisites for garnering enthusiastic support. In addition, private property—intellectual and real—must be fully protected. The new rule makers also want to see risk-taking, hard work, and savings and investment encouraged. Finally, they want to invest where citizens take personal responsibility seriously and where all are rewarded for their successes and held accountable for their failures.

The second group of laws and regulations is aimed at discouraging government handouts, bureaucracy and red tape. Ideally, subsidies, tariffs and taxes are reduced or eliminated and corruption, bribes and other forms of unethical and illegal behavior are punished to the greatest extent possible. Finally, debt, deficits and other examples of a country living beyond its means have to be severely constrained to prevent creation of an inflationary bias or conditions for future insolvency.

Both the IVs and MNCs are interested, at least in theory, in maximizing individual freedom and responsibility and minimizing government control. Such conditions allow our gruesome twosome maximum maneuverability and provide assurance that they will be able to reap satisfactory profits from their investments. Obviously, no country offers the full panoply of desired characteristics; those countries that come the closest or are moving fastest in the "right" direction get first crack at the money needed to grow their economies. The others are forced to limp along until they see the light or are reconciled to march to the beat of a different drummer.[7]

Where's the Beef?

Spurred by a decade of mounting economic integration, millions of jobs have been created throughout the world. Trillions of dollars in loans and investments have been transferred from rich to poor nations, resuscitating moribund economies and repositioning them for growth. Technological innovations, most notably in the medical and communications field, have improved the quality of life for much of humanity. The human life span is increasing and educational opportunities are more abundant than ever. So where's the beef?

Simply following a free market approach does not automatically lift all boats nor solve all problems. Overzealous competitors have caused severe damage to the ecosystem and MNCs have (knowingly or not) allowed their products to be made in hellish sweatshops and or sold in numerous unseemly ways. Thus opinions are sharply divided on the merits and integrity of the globalization process. While many applaud its virtues and efficacy, others justifiably claim they have been disadvantaged. The latter group complains that even when benefits are derived they have been grudgingly dispersed and inequitably shared.

Economic, Political or Party Animal

The World Economic Forum is an annual affair. Normally based in Davos, Switzerland, it attracts political, economic and social leaders from around the world. To pay tribute to the victims of September 11, 2001, the Forum gathered in New York City in 2002. As usual, this eclectic group of celebrities deliberated over the most pressing problems of the millennium: from the spread of terrorism to the significance of our shrinking global village. While some described the atmosphere as a bit festive, a great deal of soul searching took place and many provocative discussions ensued. At the same time the World Social Forum—an anti-globalization conference—convened in Porto Alegre, Brazil. At the Brazilian conference speaker after speaker passionately expounded on the dangers of the current capitalistic model. They argued that the international system of patent, copyright and trademark protection favored the industrialized nations and multinational corporations over the poor and that intellectual property rules, as adopted in 1995 by the

World Trade Organization, constrain the flow of medicine, agricultural seeds and computer software to the downtrodden of the world. Other speakers railed against the developed countries protecting their agricultural and textile industries through tariffs and government subsidies. Such actions, they claimed, hamper the natural movement of jobs to low-wage nations and, therefore, keep poorer countries from fully participating in the global economy.

Speaking at the New York conference, Bill Gates, chairman of Microsoft Corporation, warned the audience that the terms of international trade favored the developed world, creating disparities that feed resentment. "People who feel the world is tilted against them will spawn the kind of hatred that is very dangerous for all of us. I think it's a healthy sign that there are demonstrators in the streets. They are raising the question of, 'is the rich world giving back enough?'"[8]

It should be no surprise that those benefiting the most from globalization want to push it further and faster while those harmed or only getting a few crumbs work tirelessly to impede the process. Each group is acting in its assumed self-interest and either misunderstanding or ignoring the other side. Yet when Bill Gates, a titan of capitalism, raises a red flag, all is not going according to the script. To confuse the matter further, an article entitled, "Privatization Foments Revolt in South Africa," describes the very aggressive free market approach taken by top officials of the African National Congress (ANC)—many of whom are former Marxists. To reach a more equitable distribution of wealth, ANC officials believe they must first expand the pot. They have concluded that global markets and foreign capital are a prerequisite for an economy robust enough to improve living standards for all its citizens. Furthermore, they don't hide the fact that difficult adjustments will be required as the economy undergoes growing pains. Seeing no good alternatives, they counsel the electorate to persevere.

According to Adam Smith, when people put their self-interest first, society is well served. He makes his case as follows:

> *Every individual is continually exerting himself to find out the most advantageous employment for whatever capital he can command. It is his own advantage, indeed, and not that of society, which he has in view. But the study of his own advantage naturally, or rather necessarily leads him to prefer that employment which is most advantageous to the society... he intends only his own gain, and he is in this, as in many other cases, led by an invisible hand to promote an end which was no part of his intention.*[9]

The invisible hand that Smith describes is none other than free market competition. Every merchant makes a living by using his own resources to produce the goods and services he believes people will want to buy. In a competitive market many private businesses vie with one another for the same buyer. When a multitude of self-interested private sellers compete, prices tend to be lower, resources are prudently conserved, and consumer desires are met as each competitor seeks to attract potential buyers. Motivated by self-interest, both individuals and businesses are naturally led to serve society.

It is easy to see why MNCs should theoretically champion free market integration and people who lose their jobs because of privatization efforts would contest it. But when a captain of industry urges caution and former Marxists want to go full speed ahead, the situation gets a bit murky. How can each of these divergent positions reflect the view of individuals who are looking out for their self-interest? In order to clarify the situation, it is vital to understand the countless factors that one considers when analyzing how his or her situation can be optimized.

Chapter Two begins an examination of how our immature and distorted beliefs create conflict and confusion. Beliefs determine behavior. It is essential, therefore, to understand the erroneous ideas that underlie today's most accepted concept of self-interest.

Notes

[1] Kenneth M. Morris, *User's Guide to the Information Age* (New York: Lightbulb Press, Inc., 1999), 122.

[2] Thomas L. Friedman, *The Lexus and the Olive Tree* (New York: Anchor Books, a division of Random House, Inc., 2000), 81.

[3] Ibid., 80–81.

[4] Jack W. Lavery, "In Pursuit of Secular Disinflation 1: Inflation Prospects for 1984—the Impact of a Strong Recovery," *Business Outlook—Interim Economic Commentary* (Merrill Lynch, Pierce, Fenner & Smith, 1983), 3–4.

[5] Bob Woodward, *The Agenda: Inside the Clinton White House* (New York: Simon & Schuster, 1994), 84.

[6] Adam Smith, *An Inquiry Into the Nature and Causes of the Wealth of Nations;* quoted in David F. DeRosa, *In Defense of Free Capital Markets: The Case Against a New International Financial Architecture* (Princeton NJ: Bloomberg Press, 2001), 137.

[7] Friedman, *The Lexus and the Olive Tree,* 105.

[8] Jim Krane, "World Economic Forum Takes Left Turn," *Yahoo! News, http://dailynews.yahoo.com*:4 February 2002.

[9] Adam Smith, *An Inquiry Into the Nature and Causes of the Wealth of Nations,* Edited with an introduction and commentary by Kathryn Sutherland, World Classics (Oxford: Oxford University Press, 1993), 292–293.

Chapter Two

MotiveAction

Few would argue with the idea that human beings act according to their perceived best interest. There is no consensus, however, about the definition or scope of this enigmatic concept. For instance, one salesperson may believe it is to her advantage to bribe an executive of a large client company. Another salesperson might find such behavior morally repugnant or legally risky and, therefore, not in her self-interest. Even if she weren't caught and punished for the bribery, her conscience would make her feel so guilt-ridden that she would have to endure great mental anguish and intolerable stress.

Here a Bribe, There a Bribe

In many cultures bribery is an acceptable business practice. Government employees in some countries make such meager salaries that bribes are encouraged to enable employees to eke out a living wage. In other countries, high-level government officials consider kickbacks a normal cost of doing

business. In December 2001, two Turkish government officials were caught on hidden cameras tucking cash in their
pockets and agreeing to accept tens of thousands of dollars
in exchange for state funding of a construction project.
Corruption in Turkey, as in many other countries, became
widespread as the government began to encourage international trade. Business people offered political connections in
exchange for kickbacks as new economic liberalization
increased opportunities to act unscrupulously. While the
Turkish government has made scores of arrests in its anti-
corruption campaign, most anti-bribery laws have gaps big
enough to drive a ten-ton truck through.[1] Until enough people understand that bribery is not only unfair but also detrimental to personal and societal development, corruption is
likely to continue unabated.

As the issue of bribery illustrates, what one person does in
any given situation is not necessarily what others will do,
even though they are both presumably promoting their self-
interest. The importance attached to various self-interest factors varies from person to person and skews each person's
behavior. Therefore, if we are to understand the motivation
underlying the countless interactions in the global economy,
it is necessary to refine this elusive concept. Scrutinizing an
individual's cognitive moral development turns out to be an
important key to this puzzle. That's a fancy way of asking,
What is the morality of the people being observed?

Stages of Morality

Readers familiar with Kohlberg's and Maslow's concepts might want to skip to the section below titled "A
Reconciliation." All others please persevere. Although a bit
academic, this background material is crucial to understanding why we behave as we do and how our behavior causes
conflicts.

Harvard psychologist Lawrence Kohlberg spent over 20 years studying the various stages through which people progress in their moral development. Kohlberg divided this development into three levels of two stages each; a total of six stages of moral development.

1. Pre-conventional level—Punishment and reward are the primary concern; there is little awareness of the needs of others. This stage is followed by awareness of the needs of others but without an understanding of the abstract ideas of right and wrong.

2. Conventional level—We seek the approval of others and submit to authority. The person who acts "properly" in order to be accepted by family and friends falls into the third stage. No moral ideal is being displayed, simply a need for acceptance. Stage four is one of law and order; complying with regulations of the authorities and the norms of society.

3. Post-conventional level—People are concerned with the common good and act according to universal principles. At the fifth stage, a person is aware of and tolerates differing views. At the sixth and final stage, a person relies on conscience and rationality to guide his actions. Universal principles of justice, equality, rights, etc. provide a moral compass.

Most individuals in Kohlberg's study reached the fourth or fifth stage of moral cognitive development by adulthood, but very few people reached the sixth stage.[2] According to Kohlberg, moral development is not correlated with intelligence; advancement through the stages of moral development is based on time, education and experience. Corporate culture and ethics training have been shown to influence the moral views of business people. Inherent in Kohlberg's research is the notion that certain levels of moral development are more advanced than others. For instance, behavior based on reciprocity—you scratch my back and I'll scratch yours—is on a lower level of moral development than values based upon universal principles, i.e., acting for the common good regardless of personal consequences. It is important to be aware that conflicts often arise when people at different stages of moral development interact.[3]

Hierarchical Needs

To comprehend fully the self-interest puzzle, we must delve further into human development. For this we turn to another famous psychologist, the late Abraham Maslow, who postulated that all people share certain primary needs that he arranged in a hierarchy of five levels. These levels are as follows:

1. Physiological needs: food, clothing, shelter and rest.
2. Safety or security needs: freedom from pain or fear of the elements and predators/competitors.
3. Social needs: belonging, giving and receiving.
4. Esteem needs: achievement, status, appreciation and respect.
5. Spiritual needs: self-development, self-fulfillment, self-realization.

Maslow believed that virtually all human thought and behavior could be explained in terms of these needs; either in attempting to meet these needs or reacting to an inability to satisfy them. These needs help determine our priorities and values and, once a particular need is met, it no longer serves as a strong motivating influence. Unlike Kohlberg, Maslow attaches no moral connotations to the levels in his hierarchy. There is, for example, a close relationship between need levels and income; in societies that are less developed economically, some citizens spend almost every waking moment attempting to acquire adequate food and shelter. (An exception exists with respect to spiritual needs where there is no apparent correlation with income.)[4]

Conflicts often arise between individuals working at different levels of the hierarchy. For instance, consider entrepreneur John Doe; he has just started a business and is understandably focused on survival and security needs. He would, presumably, be absorbed in earning as much as possible as quickly as possible. Another person, Jane Smith, who has already met the two lower needs, can focus more easily on other concerns, such as preventing pollution in the workplace. Jane may not be able to garner much support for her cause from John Doe until his more basic needs are satisfied. Dealing with environmental concerns is costly, and can therefore be a drag on current earnings; pollution problems, should they occur, are likely to be long term in nature and, therefore, of little interest to Doe when there appear to be more pressing problems.

A Reconciliation

There are definite correlations between Kohlberg's stages and Maslow's hierarchy. Both begin with a seemingly selfish focus that excludes concern for anyone else. This is accompanied by the demand that conflicts be resolved totally in one's favor; compromise is not tolerated. Each model then moves to an emphasis on the acceptance and approval of others as the primary means of achieving self-worth. Finally, both reach an integrated view that emphasizes ideals such as selflessness and the unity of life. The two models are useful in explaining the full range of human behavior as well as why individuals at the same stage of moral maturity may have different needs and, therefore, act quite differently. Conversely, individuals with the same needs may be operating at different morality levels and have a different view of what maximizes their self-interest.

In thinking about these two bodies of work, I began to see a third model. This model draws from established psychological concepts and uses deceptively simple nomenclature.

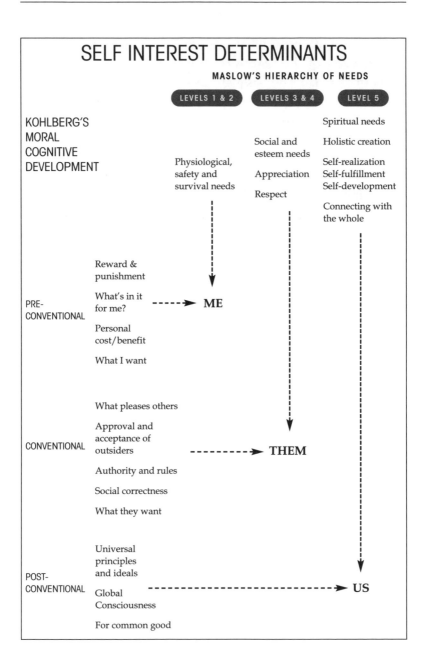

SELF INTEREST DETERMINANTS

MASLOW'S HIERARCHY OF NEEDS

LEVELS 1 & 2   LEVELS 3 & 4   LEVEL 5

**KOHLBERG'S
MORAL
COGNITIVE
DEVELOPMENT**

Physiological,
safety and
survival needs

Social and
esteem needs

Appreciation

Respect

Spiritual needs

Holistic creation

Self-realization
Self-fulfillment
Self-development

Connecting with
the whole

**PRE-
CONVENTIONAL**

Reward &
punishment

What's in it
for me?   ----▶ **ME**

Personal
cost/benefit

What I want

CONVENTIONAL

What pleases others

Approval and
acceptance of
outsiders   --------▶ **THEM**

Authority and rules

Social correctness

What they want

**POST-
CONVENTIONAL**

Universal
principles
and ideals

Global   ----------------------▶ **US**
Consciousness

For common good

The defined terms *ME* (self-centered), *THEM* (other-directed) and *US* (common-good-oriented) simply describe the characteristics attributed to these multifaceted components of our personality. Each of them gains dominance from time to time and motivates much of our behavior. (See figure on previous page for a reconciliation of the three systems.)

The simplicity of these three words requires some explanation. While there are many voices within the depths of our being, *ME*, *THEM* and *US* express the majority of our conscious and unconscious impulses. *ME* is the immature, fault prone part of us that is fearful, selfish, willful, suspicious and arrogant. This voice abhors change and, in its ignorance and laziness, is steeped in the idea that all things are separate and autonomous. **THEM** is a romanticized image of ourselves that we portray to the world in an attempt to gain acceptance and/or avoid responsibility for shortcomings. This persona blames others for its failures, is quick to judge and conceitedly thinks of itself as special. The qualities embodied by *US* include the will to love, to be in truth and to serve the best in life. It is the nonjudgmental witness that acts as our moral conscience and empowers us to discern goodness and truth without negating what others do or say. The *ME* and *THEM* part of our personality, with which we usually identify, is just a small fragment of the infinitely larger *US* component that is eternally aware of its connection to the whole. As the evolutionary process proceeds, the illusion that the world is composed of separate, discrete parts begins to fade. At the same time, the *ME* and *THEM* voices grow weaker relative to the self-realized *US*. It is at this point that we truly understand the all-encompassing nature of self-interest.

In the opening two chapters we have shown that economic integration is both a natural and inevitable process, having the potential to raise the standard of living and quality of life throughout the world. The challenge is for each of us to be supportive of the process or, to put it another way, to ensure that it satisfies our self-interest. This can happen only to the extent that benefits of globalization are perceived as equitable and sustainable. The next section, therefore, will examine the events dominating the news with an eye to identifying where and why conflicts (among *ME-*, *THEM-* and *US-*thinking) exist.

Notes

[1] Selcan Hacaoglu, Associated Press, "On Real TV in Turkey, it's Bribery in Action," *The Philadelphia Inquirer,* 8 December 2001, A2.

[2] Joseph W. Weiss, *Business Ethics: A Stakeholder and Issues Management Approach,* 2nd ed. (Fort Worth TX: The Dryden Press—Harcourt Brace College Publishers, 1998), 21.

[3] James B. Stewart, *Den of Thieves* (New York: Simon & Schuster, 1991), 63.

[4] Ian Wilson, *The New Rules of Corporate Conduct: Rewriting the Social Charter* (Westport CT: Quorum Books, an Imprint of Greenwood Publishing Group, Inc., 2000), 102.

PART TWO

THE CHALLENGES

"The dominant political and economic model today allows, indeed encourages, citizens to make the pursuit of their own interests (understood largely in terms of material wealth) the chief goal of their lives. We rarely reflect, either collectively or as individuals, on whether this dominant conception is a wise one."

PETER SINGER, AUTHOR
HOW ARE WE TO LIVE?

Chapter Three

EntrepreneurCelebs

The term "entrepreneur" originated in France around the 17th century. In French the word means someone who undertakes a meaningful activity or project. French economist Jean Baptiste Say described an entrepreneur as someone who shifts economic resources into an area of higher productivity. Joseph Schumpeter considered entrepreneurial innovation as the driving force in the creative-destructive process so necessary to a capitalist system. And Peter Drucker saw entrepreneurs as change agents who search for and exploit opportunities. Contrary to conventional wisdom, Drucker didn't consider starting a business or seeking profit to be a necessary component of being an entrepreneur.[1] The definitions provided by these well-known economists are an excellent starting point for understanding the entrepreneurial model. My knowledge of the subject, however, has been enriched by my personal experiences over the past 30 years—starting and nurturing a business coupled with observing and analyzing hundreds of entrepreneurial start-ups look-ing for investment capital.

Innovate or Perish

Many entrepreneurs start with the fervent desire to fulfill a vision that will not only benefit the entrepreneur but—through Adam Smith's "invisible hand"—society as well. An entrepreneur wants to create something new or do some-thing better, faster or cheaper. They must love what they do to devote endless time and effort to make the enterprise oper-ationally effective and financially viable. To maintain a com-petitive advantage, entrepreneurs must be fast and flexible so they can adapt to shifting conditions. They are among society's boldest risk takers. From initial vision to roller-coaster execution they often teeter on the edge of failure. As a matter of fact, risk-taking is so vital to the concept of entre-preneurship that cultures where it is encouraged usually thrive; where it isn't they whither. In California's Silicon Valley, for example, failure is a rather commonplace event. There is little, if any, notoriety attached to a bankruptcy. Some even consider it to be a valuable, if not necessary, experience. Rather than blackballing an entrepreneur who has failed, many venture capitalists consider insolvency a rite of pas-sage that enhances the likelihood of future success and, there-fore, warrants another opportunity.

To be successful entrepreneurs must hire and retain people that complement their strengths and counterbalance their weaknesses. The founder's enthusiasm for excellence and innovation must be instilled in co-workers by giving them autonomy and responsibility and making them accountable for their results. Ideally, an employee should be motivated to act as if the company were his or her own—and compensated accordingly. Rewarding employees appropriately for their successes and allowing them to experience the consequences of their failures is a vital component of building a dedicated, responsible workforce.

It becomes increasingly difficult to maintain one's passion when a company's products have achieved market acceptance and financial stability is assured. But it can be done. The keys are to establish an entrepreneurial culture based on enduring values and to maintain a competitive advantage by offering superior products and services at fair prices. Where conflicts arise, proven principles must take precedence over self-serving convenience and continuous improvement must be a priority if complacency and stagnation are to be avoided.[2]

How does a society encourage its entrepreneurs to initiate change and create wealth? Minimizing regulations and bureaucracy and encouraging risk-taking are two important elements. The most vital, however, is the willingness to destroy the old so that the new has an opportunity to thrive. Creative destruction is central to fostering entrepreneurship. Entrepreneurs are the bridge between the antiquated and the avant-garde. They can commercialize new concepts and technologies at a dazzling speed. In societies that support the status quo of entrenched, but poorly performing, businesses, powerful vested interests resist change and entrepreneurship is stifled. Cultures that hamper the continual need to tear down outmoded ways of thinking remain stuck in the past and prevent entrepreneurs from emerging.

Given the growing recognition that entrepreneurs hold the key to job creation and economic growth, governments increasingly strive to build a vibrant entrepreneurial class. We will examine this phenomenon in greater detail in ensuing chapters. This chapter concentrates on two entrepreneurial companies that initially enjoyed spectacular success followed by devastating demise. There is much to be learned from the experiences of these headline-grabbing companies.

The World to Com

In 1974, Microwave Communications Inc. (MCI) filed an antitrust suit against AT&T and, in 1980, won $1.8 billion in damages from the mother of all telecommunications companies. Four years later, a federal judge ordered the divestiture of the AT&T phone monopoly. To take advantage of the court-ordered breakup, MCI needed to build a coast-to-coast long-distance network at break-neck speed. With less-than-pristine credit ratings, MCI had to tap nontraditional funding sources to bankroll this expansion. Wall Street and its thriving junk bond business worked its magic—raising the billions of dollars MCI required. By 1987 this upstart telephone company was offering nationwide long distance telephone service; a year later it offered direct-dial service to 147 countries.[3]

In 1997, WorldCom startled the investment community by announcing a $30 billion bid to take over MCI. At the time, the deal was the largest merger in history. Little did anyone know that WorldCom would set a far less illustrious record a mere five years later. Under the leadership of chief executive officer (CEO) Bernard Ebbers and chief financial officer (CFO) Scott Sullivan, WorldCom had purchased dozens of small telecom companies over a number of years. It was the 1997 acquisition of MCI, however, that transformed WorldCom into one of the largest telephone carriers in the world. Ebbers—whose entrepreneurial career is said to have begun running an 18-room motel in southern Mississippi—soon attained star status in the media and celebrity on Wall Street. WorldCom's Board of Directors compensated him well and authorized hundreds of millions of dollars in personal loans.

Besides his full-time job as CEO of WorldCom, Ebbers was actively involved in buying, building and running several unrelated businesses.[4] The total scope of Ebber's non-WorldCom businesses was summarized in a 2002 report by WorldCom's internal auditors: a Louisiana rice farm, a luxury yacht building company, a lumber mill, a country club, a minor-league hockey team, an operating marina and a building in downtown Chicago. Ebbers chose to finance many of his acquisitions with loans secured by shares of WorldCom stock. As the value of WorldCom stock had to remain equal to or greater than the amount of the loan, this massive indebtedness left Ebbers dangerously exposed. In late 1999, the price of WorldCom stock began to decline precipitously putting his loans in a precarious position. In Ebbers' 2005 trial, the prosecution pointed to the existence of these loans as clear motive for the fraudulent practices that followed.[5]

A report commissioned by WorldCom's Board of Directors and conducted by the law firm Wilmer, Cutler & Pickering, detailed how, beginning in 1999, the company used questionable accounting to cover billions of dollars in losses. "It was when his [Ebbers] personal financial empire was under the greatest pressure—when he had the greatest need to keep WorldCom's stock price up in order to avoid margin calls that he could not meet—that the largest part of the fraud occurred." The report alleged that Ebbers participated in meetings that were held to find ways of inflating revenue. But, the report continues, "the fraud was implemented by… WorldCom's Chief Financial Officer, Scott Sullivan."[6]

Sullivan came to WorldCom through a merger in 1992 with Advanced Tele-communications Corporation. Beginning in December 1994, he served as chief financial officer, treasurer and secretary. The behind-the-scenes architect of WorldCom's many acquisitions, Sullivan is said to have devised the colossal bid for MCI—a company over three times the size of WorldCom—while flying on an airplane.[7] His base pay went from $150,000 to $750,000 plus a $3 million performance bonus, a $10 million retention bonus and stock options worth tens of millions of dollars. Sullivan built a posh $15 million house in Boca Raton, Florida and expected to spend $50,000 per year for its maintenance and upkeep.[8]

For years WorldCom reported a rapid growth in revenue. But in February 2002 it announced a reduction in its 2002 revenue and earnings projections and a massive write-down of many of its previous acquisitions. The SEC launched an inquiry into WorldCom's accounting practices shortly thereafter. At the end of April Bernie Ebbers resigned as CEO. In June 2002 a spectacular corporate fraud, involving expenses that were improperly booked as capital expenditures, was reported at WorldCom. Initially estimated at $3.8 billion, the magnitude of the loss was soon recognized to be several times larger. Sullivan was fired and David Myers, the controller, resigned. The company filed for bankruptcy in July 2002.[9]

On March 2, 2004 Sullivan pleaded guilty to federal charges and agreed to testify against Ebbers. At the same time Ebbers was indicted on charges of conspiracy to commit securities fraud, securities fraud and making false statements to regulators and investors about the company's financial condition. He pleaded not guilty.[10] On March 15, 2005, Ebbers, one of the most celebrated business executives in the 1990s, was found guilty on all nine criminal counts filed against him. His attorney indicated Ebbers will appeal and predicted he will eventually be vindicated.[11]

The WorldCom saga set several records: the largest bankruptcy in U.S. history, the largest fine ever levied against a company by the U.S. Securities and Exchange Commission and the largest acquisition ever made in the U.S.[12] Obviously, one hopes the first two records will never be broken. We now turn to a bankruptcy that, although slightly smaller, may have even greater repercussions for investors, employees and consumers. It occurred a few months before the WorldCom (since renamed MCI) filing and is likely to be cited in articles and textbooks for years to come.

A Shock Heard 'Round the World

Enron was cited by its corporate peers as the most innovative company in America for an unprecedented six years in an annual poll conducted by *Fortune*. It was the seventh largest company in the United States in terms of revenue and the second largest company ever to declare bankruptcy. Using a combination of accounting alchemy and sleight of hand gimmickry, Enron borrowed money through related entities to hide its debts. This "creative" accounting deluded investors into believing that the company was more profitable and less leveraged than was actually the case.[13]

In the mid-80s Kenneth Lay was appointed chairman and chief executive officer of Enron—the corporate entity created from the merger of two natural gas pipeline companies: Houston Natural Gas and InterNorth. In 1987 Jeffrey Skilling, a McKinsey consultant, helped Lay create the first forward contract for natural gas. In 1990 he joined Enron as a full-time employee.[14] As states across America began to experiment with deregulation of the gas and electric utility industry, Lay realized the potential for transforming energy supplies into financial instruments that could be traded like other marketable securities. Lay and Skilling were envelope-pushing entrepreneurs who believed, if they could trade energy, they could trade almost anything. The corporation made a substantial investment of time and money in strengthening their intellectual capital. They strove to make a transition from an asset- to a knowledge-based "new economy" company. With hindsight, they probably wish the company had less brain-powered assets and more mundane hard assets. By October 1999, Enron was ready to launch its Internet-based system for wholesale energy trading. In January 2000 the company detailed its plans to build a high-speed broadband telecom network and trade bandwidth;

i.e., network capacity, in the same way it traded electricity and gas. In the 1999 annual report Lay wrote, "we witnessed an acceleration of Enron's staggering pace of commercial innovation, driven by a quest to restructure inefficient markets, break down barriers and provide customers with what they want and need."[15]

In August 2000 Enron's stock hit an all-time high of over $90 representing some $70 billion in stock market value. A regrettably high percentage of Enron employee retirement plans was imprudently invested in company stock. On February 12, 2001 Skilling became president and CEO of Enron. Approximately six months later, on August 14, 2001, he resigned citing personal reasons; Lay returned as chief executive officer. Enron's global finance vice-president Sharon Watkins warned Lay in August of 2001 that accounting problems and a high level of secrecy surrounded certain Enron partnerships. Watkins wrote a note stating, "I am incredibly nervous that we will implode in a wave of accounting scandals."[16] On October 16, 2001 Enron reported a quarterly loss of over $600 million (reducing shareholder equity by $1.2 billion) due, in part, to partnerships run by then chief financial officer Andrew Fastow. A short time later, on December 2nd, Enron filed for bankruptcy and laid off 4,000 employees.

During Enron's ascendancy Fastow demonstrated his entrepreneurial talent by constructing complex partnerships called "special-purpose entities" (SPEs). Enron used these partnerships to keep debt off its financial statements without relinquishing control of the assets that guaranteed that debt. His staff grew to over 100 and he earned a reputation as a creative money maven. Fastow was so convinced of his importance that, despite the obvious conflicts of interest, he insisted—in a clear case of *"ME*-management"—on representing the interests of both Enron and its partnerships.

Although Fastow contended that he needed to be on both the buy and sell side of the SPE's to attract investors, a more plausible reason was the incredible profitability of the partnerships—allegedly earning him over $40 million.[17]

Fastow worked hard to enrich not only himself but those who could be of use to him. For example, Michael Kopper, who was a top aide of Fastow, negotiated a transaction with Fastow in which Kopper and his co-investor received more than $10 million from Enron for a $125,000 investment in one partnership.[18] Kopper became the first ex-Enron executive to plead guilty and strike a deal with prosecutors by identifying a string of partnerships set up to give a false picture of Enron's financial strength while simultaneously enriching himself, Fastow and others. Almost a year and a half later Fastow pleaded guilty to conspiracy, accepted a ten-year prison sentence and agreed to cooperate in the ongoing investigation of Enron.[19]

Energetic Politics

Enron long maintained a prominent local and national political profile. Company executives threw glitzy parties and enjoyed celebrity status across the country. They were hailed as visionaries and their pictures were prominently displayed on the covers of many of the most prestigious business magazines. A glimmer of Enron's wide-ranging political largesse came to light when the company agreed to pay $109,000 to settle allegations that it made more than 30 illegal contributions in 1999 to political candidates in New Jersey.[20] Their fall from grace—as swift as it was spectacular—shook the political establishment.

Honesty and fairness are indispensable to the long-term success of any business; transparency is essential to a smooth functioning market economy. Lay reportedly told *BusinessWeek* on August 20, 2001: "There are no accounting issues, no trading issues, no reserve issues, no previous unknown problem issues. The company is probably in the strongest and best shape that it has ever been." About ten days later, it was reported that Skilling, who had resigned as CEO on August 14th, told *BusinessWeek*, "People are afraid there's another shoe to drop, but it's just not the case." These statements seem in sharp contrast to the memo that Watkins had written on August 15th warning of a disastrous accounting deception.[21]

In February 2004 Skilling was taken to court and charged with multiple counts of fraud, insider trading and conspiracy to manipulate Enron's financial statements. According to the indictment his stock trading in Enron generated millions of dollars from April 2000 to September 2001. Skilling pleaded not guilty.[22] Lay surrendered to authorities on July 8, 2004 as the government unsealed an indictment charging him with a wide-ranging scheme to deceive regulators, shareholders and the public about Enron's financial condition. Specific charges include conspiracy, wire fraud and making false statements in connection with loans he obtained to buy shares of stock. Lay pleaded not guilty and began a persuasive public relations blitz to tell his side of the story.[23]

Lessons for Everyone

The court system will ultimately determine if Lay or Skilling are guilty of any crimes. It may be that neither of these top executives knew about the illegal activities taking place in the ranks below them and, therefore, acted both legally and reasonably. Regardless of the number of executives convicted of crimes at WorldCom and Enron, both of these Byzantine scandals provide a potent wake-up call for all of us. There are times in our lives when we have to make a choice—act only in our personal interest or for the welfare of all. When conflicts arise, *ME*-dominant personalities—and we all have this tendency to some degree—choose what serves their narrow self-interest. Anyone who places money above principle or takes advantage of a privileged position is ignoring the effect such behavior has on others. Selfish acts may seem advantageous in the short-run but it eventually becomes clear that disregarding the needs of others can never be to our advantage.

The WorldCom and Enron executives detailed above are clear examples of what Rakesh Khuranca, a Harvard Business School professor calls "Celebrity CEOs [who] focus themselves at the center of attention at an organization." Those who study successful CEOs have found that companies fare better with leaders who spurn fame and focus on the company rather than themselves.[24] The more money and power at stake, the harder it seems to make decisions that are fair and sustainable. A number of recent scandals extended well beyond corporate headquarters reaching into the offices of well-educated professionals who also succumbed to the temptation of satisfying their narrow self-interests.

Who's on Board?

Board members are beholden to management for their positions as well as their paychecks. SEC chairman William H. Donaldson noted a trend over the last decade for boards of directors to rubber-stamp the actions of "imperial" chief executives. CEOs generally want to dominate their boards; they do this by deciding what information is presented and by handing out lucrative side deals to gain the undeviating loyalty of individual members.[25] In the case of WorldCom, it has been reported that directors were given generous stock options as well as other valuable perks. One director was allegedly permitted to rent company aircraft at less than the cost of operating the plane; another director was allowed to invest in a competing suburban long-distance telephone company despite the potential conflict of interest. According to a former WorldCom director, "Ebbers treated you like a prince—as long as you never forgot who was king."[26]

Some of the directors at Enron purportedly had side deals that ranged from consulting jobs to the purchase of goods and services from affiliated companies. One Enron director was reportedly paid almost $500,000 in one year for consulting services provided to the very firm he was supposed to be overseeing. Charles Ellison, a director of the Center for Corporate Governance at the University of Delaware makes clear: "Directors who have side consulting arrangements are not considered, under governance guidelines, to have the necessary independence from management."[27] Understandably, where independence is lacking directors are less inclined to ask hard questions of management.

Greed up Top

What many consider bloated executive compensation is often cited as an example of capitalism run amok. Between 1990 and 2000, executive pay in the United States jumped 571 percent. By comparison, workers' wages increased 37 percent, barely outpacing the 32 percent inflation rate.[28] A large portion of executive compensation now comes in the form of stock options, thereby shifting the attention of management to short-term results. Executives spend an inordinate amount of time promoting, and sometimes manipulating, the stock price rather than building long-term value in the company. This tends to align the interests of executives with short-term speculators rather than long-term investors.

Fortune is one of many business publications that has featured articles on the excesses of today's executive compensation. In one such article *Fortune* reporter Carol Loomis discussed executive pay with seven high-powered executives who sit on the compensation committees of the boards of directors at several corporate behemoths. In return for the promise of anonymity, these heavyweights provided candid opinions on the state of executive pay. One, the CEO of a very successful Fortune 500 company, reportedly stated: "The scandal of what goes on in compensation is how much is paid in the many, many instances when it isn't at all deserved. But a sub-scandal is the lack of a charge against earnings when stock options are issued. Companies go along as if these things are free, when actually they cost the shareholder enormous amounts."[29]

Ira Millstein is a well-known corporate governance attorney. He advised companies such as Tyco International Ltd. and Vivendi Universal on reforming their boards after they became notorious for corporate excesses. In his view, "When I see $20 or $25 million a year, I really wonder is 500 times the factory floor wage a good number? Is 400 times? At what point in your gut does it tell you that something is out of control? Does any one human being account that much for the success of the company?"[30] Numerous prosperous companies limit executive pay to a maximum of 5 to 10 times what the lowest- paid employee earns; evidence enough that exorbitant pay is not a prerequisite for success.

Another *Fortune* interview focused on the well-paid CEO of a multinational company who served on several large corporate boards. In his view: "There is something intrinsically wrong with some of these amounts of money. I don't know that anything will stop that except self-control. But to ask for self-restraint flies in the face of human nature."[31] Hold on now! Is this the truth or a popular misconception? I believe it is the latter. Human nature is not fixed and inviolate; rather, it evolves as values and priorities change. Consider the fact that some individuals succumb to bribery and other illegal and unethical practices and others do not. The significance of our ever-evolving values will be a continuing point of discussion in the chapters that follow.

Conflicted Accounts

The purpose of financial statements is to show the economic performance and financial viability of a company. The balance sheet provides a picture of the assets, liabilities and net worth of a business at a specific point in time. The profit and loss statement shows revenue and expenses and the resulting profitability, or lack thereof. The accountants' presumed objectivity reassures those relying on the statements and gives them confidence that the figures accurately reflect the health and sustainability of the organization. In other words, the stamp of approval of the auditor is what makes financial statements credible.

Unfortunately, accountants often provide both auditing and consulting services to the business community. This creates a potential conflict of interest as the consulting services are more lucrative and, therefore, more highly prized. It is widely assumed that the better the financial numbers look—perhaps aided by less stringent audits or more liberal interpretations of accounting rules—the more pleased management will be. Logically, accounting firms believe they are then in a better position to gain consulting work if management is satisfied with their auditing work. It turns out that Enron paid now-defunct Arthur Andersen more for its consulting than for its auditing services. Andersen also audited WorldCom and a variety of other companies that ran into financial trouble. The fact that other accounting firms have had similar problems can be partly explained by the results of a recent experiment.

In a controlled experiment, 139 auditors were shown five ambiguous auditing scenarios. Half were told to assume the company they were auditing hired them and the other half that a company doing business with the firm being audited retained them. On average, participants were 30 percent more likely to judge that the accounting procedures complied with

Generally Accepted Accounting Principles if they were auditors hired by the firm. It seems that even the suggestion of a hypothetical relationship with a client creates a bias favorable to the client. Similar studies have revealed comparable self-serving prejudicial results.[32]

Management hires the accountants and can also fire them. In Europe there is a more cynical view about cozy business arrangements. According to *The Economist*, Europeans, unlike Americans, believe that any chief executive who is not power hungry when he or she takes over will soon become so.[33] As long as executives and accountants view self-interest in a narrow, *ME*-dominant manner, the public needs to remain skeptical. We can only hope that recent scandals will point up the advantages of taking a long-term, broadly based point of view.

Banking Investments

A growing economy requires investment capital; the two primary funding sources are the debt and equity markets. For these markets to function properly investors must have confidence in their ability to make informed decisions; that is, they must believe the system is fair and that pertinent information is available to all interested parties on a timely basis. Investors generally rely on brokerage houses from Wall Street to Hong Kong to provide unbiased information and recommendations based on that information. Unfortunately this does not always happen. The large investment houses earn hundreds of millions of dollars in investment banking fees from the same companies their analysts are expected to research objectively.

Documents submitted to a congressional committee investigating WorldCom disclosed an apparently systematic effort, by one of the largest brokerage houses on Wall Street, to reward Mr. Ebbers with shares in initial public offerings, which, because of their frequent profitability, were not normally available to the average investor. Over a span of several years Ebbers reportedly received 868,000 IPO shares from this firm. The same brokerage house earned millions of dollars in investment banking fees from WorldCom.[34]

An example of a close, incestuous relationship between the investment banking division of a brokerage house and Enron became apparent in November 2004. Early that month four Merrill Lynch executives were convicted of conspiracy and fraud in a deal that involved the bogus sale of an interest in power plants mounted on barges. The phony sale was transacted to inflate Enron's profits and give a false impression of Enron's financial health. At the time Enron was a lucrative client wooed by other investment banking giants. The government alleged that the four brokers agreed to participate in Enron's accounting scheme in order to entice the energy powerhouse to hire them as their investment bankers.[35]

Analyzing the Analysts

Charles Schwab, the well-known financial services firm, ran an advertisement that revived a number of disturbing memories. The backdrop for the ad is a room full of stockbrokers who are being exhorted by their manager to sell a particular investment to their clients. The ad concludes with the presumed sales manager pressing his brokers to, "put some lipstick on this pig." As absurd as the ad may appear, I have witnessed many similar situations during my frequent visits to brokerage offices over the past 30 years. In aggressive pep talks, brokers are encouraged to push often unattractive or over-inventoried stocks and bonds by offering larger than normal sales commissions. Based on my experience, a customer's suitability for a particular investment is rarely, if ever, discussed.

With some exceptions, stock brokerage security analysts have an equally dismal record of helping their firms' clients. As is well known now, but was not so obvious a few years ago, analysts often take their cues from the investment banking department of their firm. I have lost count of the number of CEOs who have told me how difficult it was to get analysts to cover their companies if they don't have any investment banking relationship with which they can "remunerate" the broker for its research. I have no doubt some executives capitulated and entered into otherwise unwarranted investment banking arrangements in order to secure research coverage. With a profound lack of objectivity and little consideration for customer interests, research analysts rarely gave negative ratings to investment banking clients of the firm.

While most CEOs are bright and conscientious, they are human and have their share of faults and failings. For many years I interviewed top executives of companies in which my clients or I had investments. Unless pushed to the wall, the CEO always portrayed the prospects of the company favorably and their stock as undervalued. My partner, who was a bit older and wiser than I, repeatedly warned me of the futility of talking to company management. I eventually got the message but it took me a great deal longer than I feel comfortable admitting.

It is hard for an investor to expect candor when there is so much money riding on a favorable opinion. In some cases, the securities analysts personally own stock in the companies they are recommending. Practices such as these destroy the integrity of the capital markets. The current situation, if left unchecked, provides anti-globalists and anti-capitalists substantial evidence that the system is inequitable and needs to be revamped. Fortunately, Enronitis and similar upheavals have caused regulators and concerned citizens to increase their vigilance.

Of course, integrity cannot be mandated nor ethics legislated. Ultimately, it is the responsibility of shareholders, not regulators, to keep the system fair, honest and efficient. The 100 largest pension and mutual fund investment managers represent the ownership interest of one-half of all U.S. equities and can wield enormous influence with corporate management.[36] But they also want to manage the retirement plan assets of the exact same companies in which they are investing. A conflict created to test one's soul! If they appear to be looking after the interests of the mutual fund holders, they risk alienating their existing and potential clients and losing the chance to win new, very lucrative business. Too often institutional investors simply sell their stock and walk away whenever news of corporate misbehavior is disclosed. In an effort to find ways to resolve this conflict, some prominent members of the investment community have taken a proactive stance on issues of full disclosure, "managed earnings," executive compensation, auditor independence and Wall Street duplicity. Jack Bogle, founder of the Vanguard Group, is promoting a "federation of long-term investors" that would place corporate values ahead of short-term stock price fluctuations.[37] Other respected money managers have echoed Bogle's call. It is time for less walking out and more speaking out!

No Monopoly Here

The unsavory sagas cited above are not an American business exclusive. Financial transgressions occur in all regions of the world:

In April 1992 Indian banks and brokers were accused of fuelling a boom on the Bombay Stock Exchange by colluding illegally to siphon $1.3 billion from the interbank securities market.

In December 1993 the German industrial group Metallgesellschaft suffered spectacular losses on energy linked derivative products forcing creditors to mount a $2.2 billion rescue.

In January 1994 a trader at Chile Copper Corporation, the world's largest copper producer, lost $175 million of company money in a financial scandal that rocked Chile.

In February 1995 Barings, one of Britain's oldest investment banks, collapsed after one of its traders racked up losses of $1.4 billion in unauthorized trades.

In June 1996 the world's biggest copper merchant, Sumitomo Corp., said it lost approximately $2.6 billion over 10 years from unauthorized copper trades.

In February 1997 National Westminster Bank, one of Britain's largest, revealed that its NatWest Markets subsidiary had suffered a $140 million loss as a result of systematic mispricing of interest-rate options over a two-year period.

In February 2002 Allied Irish Bank, Ireland's largest, revealed that a trader had defrauded the company of up to $750 million.[38]

In December 2003 the CEO of Italian dairy giant Parmalat resigned after admitting that many billions of dollars were missing apparently due to fraudulent accounting practices stretching over a decade.[39]

Do Not Throw the Baby Out

It is important to note that the offensive behavior of business executives, accountants and brokerage house employees is not evidence of a fatal flaw in capitalism. The free market economy did not collapse nor has it been replaced by another economic system. Capitalism provides significant benefits that no other system has yet to match. Capitalism is value neutral—it can be practiced in an unethical, cutthroat manner or a moral, harmonious manner. The direction taken—towards the ruthless or the cooperative—is a function of awareness, motivation and attitude. As Paul Volker succinctly put it, "Corporate Responsibility is mainly a matter of attitudes, and the attitudes got corrupted... in the 1990s."[40] As a broader view of self-interest becomes more widely reflected in the business world, employee productivity and creativity are bound to rise and customer loyalty and community cooperation will be enhanced. At the same time, the need for onerous laws and regulations diminishes. Entrepreneurs will then be free to fulfill their crucial role as builders of a vibrant business environment that can raise living standards throughout the world.

Future chapters will build the case—practically and philosophically—for cultivating a more inclusive, equitable treatment for the stakeholders of all organizations. In other words, moving from a *ME*- to an *US*-orientation.

Notes

[1] George Starcher, "Responsible Entrepreneurship," *European Baha'I Business Forum, www.ebbf.org/pdf/publications/responsibleentrepreneurship. pdf:* February 2004, 1.

[2] Larry C. Farrell, *The Entrepreneurial Age: Awakening the Spirit of Enterprise in People, Companies, and Countries* (New York: Allworth Press, an imprint of Allworth Communications, 2001), 141–143.

[3] Reinhardt Krause, "He Took on Ma Bell and Won," *Investor's Business Daily*, 7 May 2003, A3.

[4] Dennis R. Beresford, Nicholas deB. Katzenbach and C.B. Rogers, Jr., Counsel: Wilmer, Cutler & Pickering; Accounting Advisors: PricewaterhouseCoopers LLP "Report of Investigation by the Special Investigative Committee of the Board of Directors of WorldCom, Inc.," (31 March 2003): 294.

[5] Ibid., 295.

[6] Ibid., 6.

[7] Damian Wild, "Profile: Former WorldCom CFO Scott Sullivan," *Accountancy Age*, 4 July 2002.

[8] Scott Reeves, "Sullivan Pays the Price," *Forbes.Com, http://forbes.com/2005/02/16/cx_sr_0216ebbers_print.html*. 27 February 2005.

[9] Jared Sandberg, Rebecca Blumenstein and Shawn Young, "WorldCom Internal Probe Uncovers Massive Fraud," *The Wall Street Journal Online*,

http://online.wsj.com/article_print/0,SB1025044139757626480,00.html: 6 June 2002.

¹⁰ Paul Davidson, Jayne O'Donnell and Edward Iwata, "Former WorldCom CEO Ebbers Indicted," *USA Today*, 3 March 2004, B1.

¹¹ Erin McClam, "Former WorldCom CEO Guilty on All Counts," *Yahoo! News*, *http://news.yahoo.com/news?tmpl=story&cid=509&u=/ap/20050315/ap_on-bi_ge/ebbers_trial*: 15 March 2005.

¹² Larry Neumeister, "Telecom Firm Faces a Record SEC Fine," *The Philadelphia Inquirer*, 20 May 2003, E1.

¹³ Paul Solman, "Accounting Alchemy," *OnlineNewsHour, http://www.pbs.org/newshour*: 22 January 2002.

¹⁴ Wendy Zellner, "Jeff Skilling: Enron's Missing Man," *BusinessWeek*, 11 February 2002, 39.

¹⁵ Kenneth L. Lay, Jeffrey K. Skilling and Joseph W. Sutton, "To Our Shareholders," *Enron Annual Report* (1999).

¹⁶ Marcy Gordon, "Enron Head Touted Stock Amid Trouble," *Yahoo! News*, *http://dailynews.yahoo.com*: 19 January 2002.

¹⁷ Bill Saporito, "How Fastow Helped Enron Fall," *Time.Com, http://www.time.com/time/business/printout/0,8816,201871,00.html*: 28 February 2005.

¹⁸ William C. Powers, Jr., Raymond S. Troubh and Herbert S. Winokur, Jr., Counsel: Wilmer Cutler & Pickering, *Report of Investigation by the Special Investigative Committee of the Board of Directors of Enron Corp.*, (1 February 2002), 26.

¹⁹ "Chronology of Enron Corp.," *Forbes.Com, http://Forbes.Com/associatedpress/feeds/ap/2004/11/03/ap1631509.html*: 3 November 2004.

²⁰ "Enron to Pay Fine to Settle Allegations Over Political Gifts," *The Philadelphia Inquirer*, 19 July 2003, D3.

²¹ "The Post-Enron World," *BusinessWeek*, 4 February 2002, 108.

²² Kristen Hays, "Former Enron CEO Skilling Pleads Innocent," *AP Wire*, *http://www.mercurynews.com/mld/mercurynews/7984360.htm*: 20 February 2004.

²³ Dan Ackman, "Ken Lay Indicted, and Fights Back," *Forbes.Com, http://www.forbes.com/2004/07/08/cx_da_0708lay_print.html*: 8 July 2004.

²⁴ Ellen Simon, "CEOs' Fame Rarely Leads to Fortune," *The Philadelphia Inquirer*, 13 February 2005, C11.

²⁵ Marcy Gordon, "SEC May Add to Shareholder Rights," *The Philadelphia Inquirer*, 16 July 2003, D2.

²⁶ Charles Haddad, "How Ebbers Kept the Board in His Pocket," *BusinessWeek*, 14 October 2002, 139.

²⁷ Reuters, "Enron Directors' Deals Raise Eyebrows," *Yahoo! News*, *http://dailynews.yahoo.com*: 1 December 2001.

²⁸ Sarah Anderson, John Cavanaugh, Chris Hartman and others, "Executive Excess 2001: Eighth Annual CEO Compensation Survey," Institute for Policy Studies and United for a Fair Economy: 2001, 4.

²⁹ Carol J. Loomis, "This Stuff Is Wrong," *Fortune*, 25 June 2001.

³⁰ Martin Howell, "CEO Pay, Courts Now Hottest Buttons," *Yahoo! News*, *http://news.yahoo.com/news?tmpl=story2&cld=580&u=/nm/20030713/bs_nm/column_lifting*:13 July 2003.

[31] Loomis, "This Stuff Is Wrong."

[32] Max H. Bazerman, George Loewenstein and Don A. Moore, "Why Good Accountants Do Bad Audits," *Harvard Business Review* 80, 11 (November 2002), 96–102.

[33] "Corporate America's Woes Continued," *The Economist*, November 30, 2002, 61.

[34] Charles Gasparino, Tom Hamburger and Deborah Solomon, "Salomon Made IPO Allocations Available to Ebbers, Others," *The Wall Street Journal*, 28 August 2002, A1.

[35] Kristen Hays, "Five Execs Convicted in Enron Barge Case," *Yahoo! News*, *http://news.yahoo.com/new?tmpl=story&cld=530&u=/ap/20041103/ap_on*: 3 November 2004.

[36] Stewart Pinkerton, "How Deep Is the Ethics Crisis?" *Forbes.Com*, *http://www.forbes.com/2003/07/24/cz_sp_0723ethics_print.html*: 24 July 2003.

[37] Andrew Cassel, "A Prescription for Enron Syndrome," *The Philadelphia Inquirer*, 15 February 2002.

[38] Reuters, "Chronology—Previous Major Losses through Trading Upsets," *Yahoo! Finance, http://biz.yahoo.com*:6 February 2002.

[39] Gail Edmondson, David Fairlamb and Nanette Byrnes, "The Milk Just Keeps on Spilling," *BusinessWeek*, 26 January 2004, 54.

[40] Mike McNamee, "Volcker on the Crisis of Faith," *BusinessWeek*, 24 June 2002, 42.

Chapter Four

EcoIdealists

Capitalists are perceived as the most fervent globalists; EcoIdealists, also referred to as econaturalists, those most opposed to globalization. Capitalists stridently proclaim that the free market, given the chance, will resolve environmental problems and complain that government-mandated environmental regulations are inordinately time-consuming and unnecessarily costly. EcoIdealists counter that market forces are easily circumvented and often ineffective. They point to evidence that many MNCs irresponsibly exploit the earth's resources. They claim that soil depletion, toxic chemical accumulation, deforestation, greenhouse gas emissions, water contamination and air pollution are all linked to irresponsible industrial activity.

Actions that damage the environment are tolerated by those who believe effective remedies would negatively impact profits and jobs. This shortsighted approach can be traced to an economic model that separates the well-being of humans from the vitality of the world of nature. In this model, only certain things are valued. Elements of the natural world have economic value only to the extent they can be turned into desired goods and services. Clean air, fresh water and beautiful scenery are assumed to be free and can, therefore, be disregarded—destroyed and depleted in the name of economic growth. The benefits of biodiversity and the prudence of sustaining the resources of Earth for future generations are often overridden by the drive for greater profitability—now.

While environmental groups share a common purpose, there are significant differences in their sophistication and tactics. Organizations involved in the ecological movement vary from locally based conservation groups to national and international organizations involved in lobbying, research and issue-based activism. What they have in common is a recognition of the interdependence between humanity and the rest of the planet. An *US* mentality develops naturally when all life is seen as unalterably connected. Nonetheless, the extent to which environmentalists are willing to make financial and life-style sacrifices to rectify deteriorating ecological conditions varies considerably. It is, therefore, possible to categorize ecological devotees into *ME*, *THEM* and *US* subsets. *ME* environmentalists want to improve conditions but "not in my backyard." In this camp are those who oppose the building of energy efficient windmill farms because of their intrusive location. *THEM*-focused environmentalists blame others for the ecological degradation. At the same time, they continue to drive cars with less than optimum gas mileage and do little to eliminate the superfluous paper products that inundate society and take a toll on forests worldwide. I am guilty of this inconsistent behavior more times than I would like to admit. There are few purists in any human endeavor. Some individuals and organizations, however, stand out as leaders in this effort; they will be show-cased later in the chapter. First, some background on the source and scope of the inevitable conflicts and observations from organizations rethinking the current state of affairs.

Enronitis Au Naturel

REP America (Republicans for Environmental Protection) is a coalition of citizens trying to combine two seemingly incompatible interest groups—mostly right-of-center politicians and environmentalists. Their mission is to restore natural resource conservation and sound environmental protection as fundamental tenets in the platform of the Republican Party. The communications director for REP wrote an editorial in which he compared Enron's financial shell game to today's inadequate understanding of environmental degradation. The author fears that, as a society, we are not properly accounting for over-taxing the resources of the earth. When 60,000 square miles of wild tropical forest are lost every year, we don't recognize the liquidation of those assets. Rather we consider only the income generated by the timber production and mark it down as a positive addition to national output (Gross Domestic Product or GDP—the widely revered economic indicator that tallies the value of goods and services purchased by governments, businesses and households). Compare this to the manner in which Enron failed to disclose its true financial situation by reporting a variety of uneconomic, non-cash transactions as profits while obscuring its off-balance-sheet liabilities in essentially incomprehensible accounting.[1]

The environment provides essential life support services: oxygen to breathe, water purification and storage, topsoil formation and waste recycling among others. Is it not an act of self-deception when we fail to account properly for the way "natural capital" (the existing air, water, plants and solar energy from which all resources are derived) is dissipated faster than it can be replenished? The main functions of natural capital are resource production (fish, timber and crops), waste assimilation (CO_2 absorption and sewage decomposition), and life support services (UV protection, biodiversity, water cleansing). We delude ourselves by thinking all is well while we continue liquidating natural resources. At the same time liabilities such as widespread pollution and ecosystem degradation are deceivingly kept off the books and, therefore, hidden from all but the most discerning observers.[2]

Progress or Poverty

Redefining Progress (RP) is a non-profit, non-partisan public policy institute at the forefront of a progressive approach to social, economic and environmental problems similar to that of REP America. They believe the way most countries account for the income and expenditures of their citizens is significantly flawed. Specifically, that GDP does not provide an accurate picture of national economic well-being.

GDP counts only monetary transactions as economic activity, thereby omitting much that has value: services such as unpaid home care of children or elderly parents and the value of leisure time spent in rest or relaxation. Contributions derived from the environment such as clean air and water are excluded unless they're paid for; i.e., when bottled water is purchased at the supermarket. The environmental costs associated with the depletion of the natural resources used to produce goods and services are also ignored. In addition, GDP doesn't properly account for the pollution produced by economic activity. The consumption of fossil fuels, such as oil, is added to GDP even though it causes environmental damage. To compound the error, clean-up expenses associated with disasters such as the Exxon Valdez oil spill are also added to, rather than subtracted from, the GDP. These calculations violate both sound accounting principles and common sense. The depletion of natural resources must be seen for what it is—the depreciation of assets, not the augmentation of national wealth.

A Defining Moment

Redefining Progress developed the Genuine Progress Indicator (GPI) to counteract the misleading information generated by most national accounting models. The value of products and services consumed in an economy are included in GPI whether or not there is an exchange of money. In other words, GPI attempts to assess the well-being of individual citizens rather than focusing only on the amount of money they spend. In 2000, GDP in the U.S. grew by 3.9 percent. In contrast, GPI, as calculated by RP, grew by only 2.5 percent. The difference in these growth rates indicates the extent to which market prices give a false picture of the social costs of economic activity. As an example, increased fossil fuel use enhances GDP but decreases GPI. GPI accounts for increased fossil fuel use as a subtraction from national output since such use depletes natural resources, contaminates the atmosphere with a variety of emissions, increases vehicle congestion and traffic accidents and contributes to climate change. All these results have a deleterious effect on quality of life; to make them positive inputs to national accounting is, at a minimum, misleading and may lead to decisions that are not in the best interests of society.[3]

A major objective of GPI is the quantification of the growth of an economy without a corresponding decline in the stock of raw materials used for production. A decline in GPI indicates that rising consumption is being accomplished at the expense of raw material depletion. A more energy- and materials-efficient economy would expand GPI and enhance society as growth becomes more ecologically sustainable. If future generations are to enjoy the same level of natural resources available today, we must consume resources at or below the rate of replacement.

People have become complacent about their consumption patterns and, in much of the West, have been depleting resources at an unsustainable rate. In order for economic growth to be sustainable, resources cannot be turned into waste faster than nature can recycle that waste back into usable resources. To quantify the degree of consumption relative to the bioproductive potential of the planet, Redefining Progress has developed a tool for calculating the amount by which a country or region is depleting resources as a proportion of total available resources. This rather novel tool is called an "ecological footprint." The ecological footprint is defined as the land and water area needed to support a specific segment of the population using prevailing technology. It provides a comprehensive comparison of natural resource demands and the currently available supply. The footprint uses government data where available; otherwise peer-reviewed data from science literature are used. RP believes it uses conservative assumptions in calculating the footprint and, therefore, the demand on nature tends to be underestimated.[4] Other groups, such as Denmark's Environmental Assessment Institute, find the footprint approach based on questionable assumptions and, therefore, misleading. They believe this type of analysis creates an alarmist reaction that may shock people into taking unnecessary action.[5]

Is Your House Green?

There may be no more divisive issue separating free market capitalists from EcoIdealists than global warming. Global warming—also referred to as climate change and the greenhouse effect—has already had a profound effect on the globalization process and the debate is expected to get hotter. The greenhouse effect occurs when gasses such as carbon dioxide (CO_2) and chlorofluorocarbons (CFCs) absorb the infrared energy that naturally returns to the atmosphere. When these gasses become concentrated in the atmosphere they block the normal movement of heat from the surface of the earth and the temperature of the planet rises. Many business and government leaders in the U.S. believe the evidence of global warming is inadequate to justify changing the way we live and work. EcoIdealists, along with many in the scientific community, believe the evidence is more than sufficient to warrant immediate action.

The 1997 Kyoto Protocol was developed to address the growing concerns that global warming would create significant harm. In November 2001, delegates from 165 countries agreed on rules for implementing the agreement by requiring some 40 industrialized nations to limit carbon emissions or reduce them below 1990 levels. Prior to the industrial revolution, atmospheric carbon dioxide levels were between 190 and 280 parts per million by volume. More recently they were about 370 parts per million and rising by 1.5 parts per million by volume annually. Many scientists fear that, if this trend is allowed to continue, coastal flooding, more damaging droughts and volatile crop yields may result.[6]

The response of many IVs and MNCs is that, while the level of carbon dioxide has increased due to human activity, the effect of greenhouse gases on the climate is uncertain at best. Until the exact effects are known, they believe major changes are unnecessary. Why undergo costly structural changes that could adversely affect the strength of the economy and the vitality of the job market? The U.S. has long rejected the accord based on its belief that the treaty would be harmful to U.S. business and is inequitable because it excuses heavily polluting developing countries, such as India and China, from meeting the same emission level standards.

Chinese Checkers

Interestingly, one of the questions I was asked most frequently at the conclusion of my lectures in China was whether I agreed with the position of the Bush administration on the

Kyoto Protocol. I answered in much the same way that I responded to a similar question posed in an interview that was widely disseminated in the Chinese press.

> *Environmental problems, which can never be confined to national borders, can only be solved if all countries work in a cooperative manner. Thus I believe U.S. law-makers were wrong to reject the Kyoto Protocol in favor of an independent course of action. This is not to say that the specific proposals agreed to in the Kyoto pact are as effective or equitable as possible. Citizens of all countries must make sacrifices and it is always difficult to decide how the burden should be shared. In fact, environmental problems can only be solved if everyone takes personal responsibility for reducing their own waste and pollution. In addition, the clean-up process can be quickened if citizens patronize companies following responsible environmental policies while boycotting those acting irresponsibly.*[7]

Adjustments have to be made, but the sacrifices are not nearly as draconian as some would have us believe. More fuel-efficient cars don't have to affect the speed of travel or the availability of creature comforts. And while more money will have to be spent on R & D to produce more energy-efficient appliances and better-insulated windows and doors, the payback should be fast as more environmentally sensitive consumer demand spurs business to provide fuel-efficient technologies.

Looks Can Be Deceiving

I was an investment analyst in the early 1970s shortly after the Clean Air and Clean Water Acts became law in the U.S. Reflecting upon the prevailing opinion, I expected investment returns to be under pressure for many years as corporate expenditures on environmental remediation hindered profitability. L. F. Rothschild and Company, a well-respected stock brokerage firm, issued a report in late 1970 discussing the ways in which efforts to improve the environment would lead to a shift in resources from goods production to quality-of-life improvements. Their report stated, "Thus businesses may find it harder to gain funds from financial institutions as they are increasingly placed under pressure to finance environmental changes."[8] In fact, in the past three decades there has been little, if any, slowdown in economic growth attributable to the 1970s environmental laws. The reason for this unexpected outcome is that heightened environmental standards encouraged innovations that lowered costs, improved quality and spurred more energy-efficient products, all of which enhanced corporate global competitiveness. The evidence strongly suggests, therefore, that the benefits derived from cleaning up the environment outweigh the costs incurred.

Taking the Initiative

The U.S. rejection of the Kyoto Protocol notwithstanding, many U.S. corporations are taking voluntary steps to limit the emission of greenhouse gases. They realize it is in their interest to take the lead, as they will enjoy a significant advantage when limits on greenhouse emissions are widely enforced. Furthermore, by taking action now, they enhance their reputation with customers for years to come. The Business Roundtable, a prestigious business organization composed of leaders from blue chip U.S. corporations, proposed a variety of solutions to the global warming problem in a report entitled "Unleashing Innovation; the Right Approach to Global Climate Change." Ernest W. Davenport, chairman and chief executive of Eastman Chemical Company and the chair of the Business Roundtable's environmental task force said that the report "represents the business community's interest in being part of a solution to concerns about global climate change."

Other corporate giants such as Ford Motor, General Motors, Royal Dutch Shell, and BP Amoco—companies that might be impacted by limits on greenhouse gas emissions—have joined the effort to curb global warming.[9]

In mid-2004, attorneys general from eight states—Connecticut, New Jersey, New York, Rhode Island, Vermont, California, Iowa and Wisconsin—filed a federal lawsuit against five large energy companies alleged to have contributed to global warming by emitting excessive carbon dioxide. These five utilities collectively release 650 million tons of carbon dioxide per year, which equates to about 10 percent of the national total and one quarter of the carbon dioxide output of U.S. utilities. According to the lawyers, science has demonstrated that global warming contributes to a multitude of problems. Adverse results include everything from asthma to soil erosion; widely diverse industries such as farming and tourism are negatively affected. The suit demands that each company cap its emissions and reduce them by a specified percentage for a minimum of ten years. According to Connecticut Attorney General, Richard Blumenthal, "We're here because the Federal government has abdicated its responsibilities." While the suit may not prevail in court, it will certainly bring attention to an issue where voluntary actions, in the opinion of many, have been woefully inadequate.[10]

Idealism vs. Pragmatism

Global warming is beginning to have an impact in unexpected places. Zurich-based insurer Swiss Re is one among a number of insurance companies that issue directors-and-officers (D&O) liability policies that protect the directors of a company from personal liability if they are sued for mismanagement. The insurer is considering denying coverage to companies it believes are not sufficiently involved in reducing their output of greenhouse gases. Many MNCs have factories in countries that have signed the Kyoto Protocol; they are, therefore, exposed to financial and legal risks in countries where the treaty is in force. Baxter International, which gets some of its D&O insurance from Swiss Re, has recognized the consequences of ignoring the global warming issue and is one of many international companies that has voluntarily moved to reduce greenhouse gas emissions.[11]

John Browne, CEO of BP Amoco, at a speech given at Harvard University, stated that, despite the provisional nature of the science of climate change, doing nothing was not a viable option.

> *That's why we set our own targets—to reduce our own emissions of greenhouse gases by 10 per cent below the 1990 [levels]—a target we've now achieved at no net cost. It's why we're now moving to set a new objective— of stabilizing our net emissions at the new lower level over the next decade despite a possible doubling in the volume of products sold by the company, through effi- ciency and through the development of low carbon prod- ucts which offset emissions.[12]*

Environmentalists tend to be idealistic. Sometimes unre- alistic in their expectations and impractical in their approach, their strident expressions of principle are nevertheless invalu- able; they offer a different—often insightful—point of view. Eventually, idealist passions must be channeled into creative, entrepreneurial thinking if complicated ecological problems are to be solved. The sections that follow highlight two organizations that have come up with enlightened yet prag- matic approaches to resolving some intractable environ- mental problems. By focusing on the common good—*US-* dominant—they provide strong evidence that the challenges involved in changing beliefs and behaviors are more than offset by the positive returns.

A Natural Step for Humanity

I really didn't know what to expect as I entered the meeting room for an all-day "The Natural Step" (TNS) Seminar. I had a superficial understanding of this scientifically based approach to planning for ecological sustainability, but I wanted to learn more. TNS principles have gained enthusiastic acceptance from some very traditional international corporations—McDonalds, Ikea, Home Depot and Electrolux, to name a few. As I met a number of the other workshop participants, I was surprised by their diverse backgrounds. In addition to the usual cadre of dedicated environmentalists, there were business executives, religious leaders and local government officials. There was also a broad cross-section of working men and women. To my left was a veterinarian, to my right a change-management consultant, and behind me were a high school gym teacher and a stockbroker. Some came because they were curious, others because they were already committed. The instructor, Terry Gips, a graduate of the Yale School of Management, has a varied background that included stints at the White House and jobs at several large corporations. He is President of the non-profit Alliance for Sustainability and is one of a handful of individuals who have been trained by TNS to teach its principles and concepts.

Launched in 1989, TNS was the creation of Dr. Karl-Hendrik Robèrt, a Swedish physician and cancer researcher. Robèrt was concerned about rising cancer rates among children and convinced that the causes were connected to environmental factors. He began a dialogue with his fellow researchers in an attempt to determine the conditions for planetary sustainability. After 21 drafts of the original thesis,

Robèrt achieved a consensus among 50 leading Swedish scientists on the underlying principles. A major educational campaign was launched in Sweden to convince large corporations to support the findings. Since then more than 60 corporations in Sweden have implemented the principles and TNS has affiliated organizations in many countries stretching from Australia to Canada.

TNS framework is based on a dynamic assessment of economic, social and ecological factors and their associated effects on society. Gips meticulously described how, since the beginning of the industrial revolution, humanity has been violating certain basic rules of nature. At this rate, it will not be long before environmental conditions will make the earth uninhabitable. A meeting of 21 leading American scientists and engineers "agreed that the problems addressed by The Natural Step are of paramount importance to the sustainability of human civilization and its biotic underpinnings."[13]

From Despair to Hope—Step by Step

The Natural Step provides practical tools for assessing decisions that impact the sustainability of resources. The U.N. World Commission on Environment and Development defines sustainability as development that meets the needs of the present without compromising the ability of future generations to meet their needs. Interactions between human beings and the planet need to be based on an understanding that life is supported by natural processes, such as capturing energy from the sun by photosynthetic organisms and the purification of air and water. Tragically, societies throughout the world are systematically altering the structures and functions of the ecosystem in a manner that diminishes its life-supporting services. Specifically, oil, coal and a variety of minerals are mined and dispersed at a faster rate than they are deposited back into the earth's crust. Hazardous substances, such as PCBs, DDT and dioxins are produced faster than natural processes can break them down. Society extracts resources, by harvesting trees or fish, at a faster rate than they can be replenished. In an effort to counter the serious deterioration in life-supporting systems and structures, TNS defined four principles for maintaining critical ecological processes and recognizing the profound impact human behavior has on ecosystems. (These principles are described in detail on the organization's website: *http://www.naturalstep.org/learn/principles.php*)[14]

Acknowledging the problem is only the first step. Applying this understanding to everything we take from, make with, and do to our natural resources is the second. Specific actions we can take include: reducing our consumption whenever possible, using less material to make the same products, reusing and recycling whatever we make, redesigning things so they can be disassembled and reused in the future, composting and allowing inorganic material to resume its natural cycle and substituting non-toxic for toxic material.

Back at the seminar, a deepening gloom seemed to spread as Gips painstakingly detailed the scope and severity of the planet's ecological destruction. We almost began to see some truth in Woody Allen's facetious quip: "More than any time in history, humankind faces a crossroads. One path leads to despair and utter hopelessness, the other to total extinction. Let us pray that we have the wisdom to choose correctly." The mood soon shifted to cautious optimism as Gips described how, after embracing TNS, a wide variety of businesses and municipalities have been able to revitalize the ecosystem while simultaneously improving their financial vitality. From the numerous examples cited, one of the world's largest furniture manufacturers and retailers has been chosen because of its exceptionally instructive and inspiring experience.

An Ikea Whose Time Has Come.

Ikea is a highly successful MNC with worldwide sales in excess of $10 billion and more than 40,000 employees in 28 countries. With approximately 2300 suppliers in more than 64 countries the company faces the full panoply of business problems. Beginning in the 1980s, Ikea was criticized for a variety of environmental issues: packaging waste, the use of PVC plastic and the number of trees felled each year to produce their catalogue. In 1992, tests conducted by an investigative team from a large German newspaper and television station determined that formaldehyde emissions from Ikea's most popular bookshelf were higher than allowed by German law. The direct costs to track the bookshelves and correct the problem exceeded $6 million; the costs in diverted manpower, foregone sales, lost production by suppliers and the money and time required to regain customer loyalty were inestimable.

For practical as well as philosophic reasons, Ikea knew that it must examine its stand on environmental issues. It also knew that it could not do so alone and asked Dr. Karl-Hendrick Robèrt, whose reputation for balanced environmental thinking had been growing, to advise the company. After recognizing that some 3 million cubic meters of future waste was being distributed annually through sales of their products, management began to reconceptionalize and redesign the relationship between Ikea and the environment using TNS framework. They identified five key problem areas and developed policies to integrate environmental awareness into their business dealings.

1. They had to learn how the materials in their products affected health and the environment. All products were evaluated based upon their adherence to the four system principles. Ikea then decided to design furniture around the concepts of dematerialization

and disassembly. They are now recycling material from discarded furniture and using that material for new products.

2. Approximately 75 percent of the material in Ikea's products, packaging and catalogues comes from trees; the goal is to use only wood products from sustainably managed forests.

3. Many of Ikea's 2,300 suppliers are in countries with lower environmental standards than those in Western Europe or North America. Ikea's policy is to apply the strictest vendor standards found anywhere in the world to each specific component in their entire product line.

4. Ikea is a very transport-dependent company. They are working in close cooperation with their carriers to reduce the environmental impact of transport and use rail and combined road-rail transportation whenever possible.

5. Energy used to light, heat and cool retail outlets needed to be analyzed and controlled. All stores now conduct inventory audits to determine the through-put of material and energy; new Ikea stores are built with this information in mind. Annual savings from the reductions in lighting and air-conditioning, as well as lower lighting maintenance costs exceed half a million dollars.[15]

The relationship between Ikea and TNS has resulted in a number of significant benefits to the company. It has helped bring a high level of awareness and enthusiasm for environmental issues to all employees. The Natural Step framework has forced Ikea to look at its products and operations objectively. The resulting innovations serve all stakeholders and substantially improve the sustainability of natural resources.

Neither Black nor White

Capitalists are absolutely correct in complaining about the time and money expended to comply with regulations and deal with the government bureaucracies enforcing the environmental laws of every nation. EcoIdealists are equally right to point out how many industry practices cause incalculable damage to our ecosystem and threaten natural resource sustainability. The problem is to move from focusing solely on getting products to the consumer as quickly and cheaply as possible to a broader, *US*-oriented view that acknowledges the need for both financial viability and a healthy, sustainable natural world. The good news is that an increasing number of people are successfully meeting this challenge; we will look at more of them in the final section of the book.

In the meantime, the next chapter looks at the third of our protagonists—politicians. Our political servants (an oxymoron to some) are usually at the center of most global conflicts; understanding the motivation for their conduct is crucial to creating a more harmonious global community.

Notes

[1] Jim DiPeso, "Keep Better Account of the Environment," *The Philadelphia Inquirer*, 22 April 2002, A11.

[2] Ibid.

[3] "Why Bigger Isn't Better: The Genuine Progress Indicator," *Redefining Progress, http://www.rprogress.org/projects/gpi/updates/gpi1999.html*: 8 May 2002.

[4] Ibid.

[5] "Treading Lightly," *The Economist*, 21 September 2002, 74.

[6] Committee on the Science of Climate Change, Division on Earth and Life Studies, National Research Council, *Climate Change Science: An Analysis of Some Key Questions* (Washington, D.C.: National Academy Press, 2001).

[7] Xiaohua Wang, "An Interview with David A. Schwerin, Ph.D.," *Readers Guidance Weekly*, trans. Zhihe Wang (Beijing), May 2002.

[8] Paul S. Nadler, *Questions on a Capital Short Decade*, (L.F. Rothschild and Co., October 1970).

[9] Paul Raeburn, "Global Warming: Look Who Disagrees with Bush," *BusinessWeek*, 23 April 2001, 67.

[10] Emily Lambert, "Spitzer Strikes Again," *Forbes.Com, http://www.forbes.com/energy/2004/07/21/cz_el_0721power.html*:21 June 2004.

[11] Jeffrey Ball, "Insurers Weigh Moves to Cut Liability for Global Warming," *The Wall Street Journal Online, http://onlinewsj.com/article/0,SB105225191333266400.00html*:7 May 2003.

[12] John Browne, speech at Harvard University, 3 April 2002, "Leading Toward a Better World?" *GreenMoneyJournal, http://www.greenmoneyjournal.com/page.mpl/1.html*:7 May 2002.

[13] "Leading American Scientists Support TNS Principles," *Compass: The Newsletter of The Natural Step*, Vol. 1, No. 3, Spring 1997, 1.

[14] "The Natural Step Four System Conditions," *The Natural Step, http://www.naturalstep.org/framework/framework_conditions.html*:3 June 2002.

[15] The Natural Step: Organizational Case Summary (IKEA).

Chapter Five

PoliticalShortimers

- Cut income taxes 5 percent within months—by a third within five years.
- Decrease corporate taxes to the European Union average.
- Reduce the Value Added Tax (VAT) on selected items from 19.6 percent to 5.5 percent.
- Increase police on the beat—provide them with better equipment.
- Establish more prison-type institutions for young criminals.
- Create subsidies to help the young and women find jobs.

According to *The Economist,* these are a few in a long list of promises made by President Jacques Chirac of France in the months leading up to his 2002 re-election.[1] Never mind that paying for these pledges conflicts with France's budget balancing commitment to the EU—an obligation the government repudiates now that it can't deliver what was promised. Pledging more than can be delivered is standard operating practice for democratically elected politicians around the world.

Obvious—once we realize the paramount aim of political aspirants is to get elected and, once ensconced in office, retain that position or move to one with more power and authority. Politicians enthusiastically embrace the mantra "promise all things to all voters." This inevitably leads to pandering to vocal and powerful special interest groups whose objectives often conflict with the best interests of the electorate. It also means focusing almost entirely on the present and ignoring adverse consequences down the road.

As a result, the bookkeeping practices followed by most governments are often less accurate and more misleading than Enron's. Future liabilities for such things as national retirement and health benefits go largely unreported and blithely ignored. The difference between the present value of future obligations and the revenue required to fund them is enormous. To avoid hard choices and obfuscate looming problems many governments presuppose large future tax increases to cover exploding deficits. The generational imbalance that would be created is patently unfair and naively unrealistic—future taxpayers will surely rebel. If elected officials continue their irresponsible fiscal practices, eventually the problem implodes and leaves citizens in the same position as Enron's employees and stockholders—out of work, out of money and out of luck!

The impact of the government sector on an economy—through its taxation, spending and regulation—is enormous. Using influence to create and maintain a vibrant economy should be one of a politician's highest priorities. In actuality, because of self-centered career ambitions and short time horizons to the next election, politicians often promote policies that favor special interest groups over the well-being of the majority of its citizens. Nowhere is this seen as clearly as in the international trade arena.

Free Trade

An article of faith for most economists is that expanding international trade speeds economic growth. The globalization of trade has brought with it a worldwide expansion of wealth that has improved the standard of living of many countries faster than would have occurred without it. Unrestricted trade allows countries to specialize in industries where they have a competitive advantage and thereby generate higher living standards for the citizens. Since 1989 world exports have more than doubled leading to an increase of $12.3 trillion in world GDP growth.[2] Despite considerable evidence confirming the benefits of free trade, a variety of groups passionately oppose the liberalization of international trade. Opposition groups include labor unions, whose members hold the unskilled jobs most vulnerable to low wage competition; environmentalists, who fear increased pollution that accompanies industrialization; and social activists, who are concerned about the unfair distribution of benefits. Some of these criticisms are subsiding—the liberal-leaning aid agency Oxfam International praised international trade as a potential boon to the poor throughout the world. Kevin Watkins, a senior policy advisor for Oxfam states, "The extreme element of the anti-globalization movement is wrong. Trade can deliver much more [for poor countries] than aid or debt relief. History makes a mockery of the claim that trade cannot work for the poor"—some of the most prominent examples being the nations of East Asia, where, "since the mid 1970s, rapid growth in exports has contributed to a wider process of economic growth which has lifted more than 400 million people out of poverty."[3]

A study by the Fraser Institute in Vancouver, Canada confirms that countries with the fewest restrictions on trade had the highest growth in GDP from 1990 to 2000. Ranked by freedom of trade, countries in the top fifth had average annual per-capita GDP growth (adjusted for inflation) of 2 percent, while the bottom fifth had a meager 0.2 percent rate of growth. The top quintile had an average per capita GDP of $23,401 in 2000—more than twice that of the second quintile and more than six times that of the bottom fifth of countries with the most restrictive trade policies.[4]

Trading in an Interconnected World

The World Trade Organization (WTO) is the successor to the General Agreement on Tariffs and Trade (GATT), which was established over 50 years ago. The organization was developed through a series of negotiations among more than 140 member countries accounting for over 90 percent of international trade. Recognizing the enormous benefits of free trade, these countries came together to ensure the free, equitable and predictable flow of goods and services across all continents. The first negotiating rounds of GATT dealt primarily with tariff reductions while later sessions included anti-dumping rules and non-tariff measures. The Uruguay Round that created the WTO took place between 1986 and 1994. Negotiations continued and subsequent agreements have been reached on telecommunications, information technology products and financial services.

The WTO rules—the agreements—are based on a nondiscriminatory trading system that specifies the rights and obligations of members. Each country receives guarantees that its exports will be treated fairly and consistently among those of its trading partners. The WTO has established elaborate procedures for resolving trade disputes between and among countries. These procedures are critical for maintaining transparency and for enforcing agreements and ensuring the smooth flow of trade. More than three-quarters of the members are developing or less developed countries. Special provisions for these members include longer time horizons for phasing in rules at accession, greater flexibility in implementing agreements and commitments and support in building infrastructure, handling disputes and implementing technical standards.

Included among the objectives of the World Trade Organization are: optimal use of natural resources, sustainable development and environmental protection. To meet these goals, member countries are permitted to provide environmental protection subsidies; WTO rules, however, prohibit actions to protect the environment that would be discriminatory. In other words, a country cannot be indulgent with its own producers and strict with similar imported goods and services. In addition, specific provisions enable governments to take actions that protect human, animal and plant life. These actions can't, however, be used as an excuse for protecting domestic producers.[5]

A continuing goal of WTO negotiations is to effect significant reductions in industrial and agricultural subsidies leading to a decrease in wasteful overproduction. The situation in the world fishery industry is an excellent example of how trade liberalization can transform policies that threaten the environment. According to the Progressive Policy Institute, overcapacity in the world fishing fleet results in a steep decline of fish stocks; worldwide subsidies of approximately $15 billion only make the situation worse. In 1998 the U.S. and seven other countries proposed that WTO members agree to eliminate subsidies to their fishing fleets and, in spite of resistance from Japan and Europe, the subject is under serious discussion.[6] As trade barriers fall, however, previously protected producers and their workers face new competition that can lead to job losses and even bankruptcies. The WTO recognizes the seriousness of this problem and allows countries time to make adjustments. When these dislocations are especially damaging, there are provisions in the agreement that allow countries to take contingency actions against imports. Considered in total, liberalized trade between nations has clearly boosted economic growth. Almost all studies conclude that, since World War II, millions of people have been raised from poverty as a result of an increase in international trade.

The WTO has no dearth of critics. Complaints range from favoritism towards big business to a bias against developing countries and the environment. Proponents counter that corporations are given no special role in the decision-making process and pronouncements of the WTO are not binding on member states. A country can enact any regulation it chooses; the WTO merely stipulates that nations injured by a policy have the right to respond in kind. While there are arguments to be made on both sides of the environmental debate, it is hard to refute the fact that incentives exist for manufacturers to move production to countries with lower environmental standards.

Critics do, on balance, raise legitimate concerns about the WTO and the regrettable effect some policies have had on communities worldwide. The WTO will ultimately be judged on whether the benefits derived from its policies outweigh the costs and the degree to which assistance can be provided to those who suffer from the resulting dislocations.

Protect Me from Myself

The ink on the Doha WTO declaration was hardly dry when the Bush administration disclosed it was taking a number of perplexing actions, two of which involved the steel and agricultural industries. They were baffling because they were contrary to what purportedly conservative, free-traders would be expected to do. But they become much less bewildering when understood in a political context where earning the support of special interest groups is paramount. Convoluted, inconsistent policies that are economically indefensible and that jeopardize the long-term interests of the majority of citizens can still take precedence when there is an election to be won. In short, free traders be damned; PoliticalShortimers prevail again. A look at the steel and agricultural decisions will shed light on what happens when political delusions and economic reality collide.

The Protection Racket

On March 6, 2002 President Bush agreed with the International Trade Commission finding on steel dumping in the U.S. and decided to shield American steelworkers from international competition by imposing tariffs of up to 30 percent on foreign steel. Less than a year prior to this decision, on May 7, 2001 in remarks to the Council of the Americas, Bush emphatically stated, "opened trade is not just an economic opportunity, it is a moral imperative." This decision to shield the steel industry from competition is a blatant protectionist policy and a clear example of how easy it is for politicians to put politics before principles whenever politically expedient. Before analyzing the reasoning, flawed as it is, a bit of historical perspective is needed.

United States protectionist policies date back to at least the first decades of the 20th century. At that time, producers of clothing and shoes, whose output dominated the manufacturing sector, secured tariffs of as high as 90 percent to protect their products against those made by their European rivals. Despite the fact that trade protection has been unable to save jobs (apparel employment has fallen by 50 percent in the past decade alone) supporters of protectionism have been resolute in fighting for tariffs. Contrast this with the position of the newer high-tech industries that see exporting as the key to their success. Understandably, Silicon Valley has pushed to lower or eliminate all tariffs. The net result is a U.S. tariff system that is complex, inconsistent and riddled with contradictions.

Most other countries have equally counterproductive protectionist policies. The European Union has tariffs not only on clothing and shoes but heavily subsidizes its agricultural sector. Japan's policies with regard to import restrictions on cars and rice are well documented. Even developing countries which are the most vociferous in their denunciations of the protectionist policies of other nations are often found discriminating against the homegrown products of their neighbors. India, for example, not only imposes extremely high tariffs but also has an outright ban on a variety of consumer products. Consequently, India's neighbors export more to the United States than they do to India. Nepal, a country surrounded on three sides by India and the fourth side by the Himalaya, exported $220 million worth of goods to the United States in 2000 and only $177 million to India.[7]

The Steel Trap

Until the late 1970s, the steelworkers union was able to demand high wages and retirement benefits for its members through tough bargaining with an industry that repeatedly acquiesced to the demands of labor. As a result, U.S. steelworkers, who earned 15 percent more than the average manufacturing wage in 1950, were earning 84 percent more by 1980. In addition, hourly employment costs in the steel industry had risen at an annual rate of 12.1 percent from 1967 to 1979 while output grew at a mere 2 percent. It should be no surprise, therefore, that steelworkers would be concerned about the security of their jobs once imports of low-cost foreign steel began to rise. Both the union and management realized that the only way to survive in their bloated condition was to restrict low-cost foreign steel. While the steel industry received some assistance from the Reagan administration, foreign competition was only mildly subdued.

Consequently, employment in the U.S. steel industry has fallen from around 600,000 in 1980 to less than 200,000 today.[8]

With this background, it is easy to see why the Bush administration received intense lobbying from both the steel industry and congressional members in steel producing states. When jobs are at stake people quickly become political activists to protect their livelihood. Bush's decision, his advisors argued, could affect U.S. congressional elections as well as the President's own re-election chances in the crucial steel-making states. As an alternative to imposing tariffs, the administration could have provided direct assistance to fund the inordinately high health and pension benefits of steel industry retirees. These so-called "legacy costs" were negotiated when the industry was in its glory days. They are now a major impediment to the ability of unionized steel companies to sell competitively priced steel. But these costs would be an explicit budget item that would add to the national deficit in a very visible way. It was already becoming difficult for the Republicans to make the fiscal responsibility case; incurring additional obligations would make it that much harder. The damage inflicted by protectionist tariffs, while far larger than the legacy costs, is hidden from all but the most discerning members of the electorate. What are some of the costs that the administration so blithely ignored or glibly rationalized?

1. Tariffs may slow needed industry consolidation, as firms that would be forced into bankruptcy or mergers are now able to hobble along for a few more years. Tariffs, therefore, provide a false sense of safety that delays some immediate pain but leads to greater pain in the future. Tariffs do not address the real problem of high costs, most of which can be attributed to past management indiscretions and overly generous labor pacts when the industry was in its ascendancy. Thus, tariffs notwithstanding, bankruptcy cannot and should

not be averted in an industry where worldwide over-capacity is a significant problem.

2. Tariffs are taxes levied on imports that particularly hurt low- and moderate-income people. It is both ironic and hypocritical that the Bush administration has adamantly insisted that Congress not raise taxes (or at least not taxes that will be obvious). Moreover, by increasing "taxes" on the raw material of big steel users the cost of everything from cars to appliances is pushed higher and, within a short time, the prices paid by consumers rise while availability declines. Just a few months after steel tariffs were imposed, for example, Honda Motor Co. began airlifting carbon sheet steel from Japan to its U.S. plants in order to counter-act tight supplies and higher costs. Meanwhile, higher prices and increased demand for domestic steel forced auto-parts manufacturers Delphi and Dana to con-template shutting down some of their plants. "It's a huge problem and we're hearing about a lot of avail-ability problems for many types of steel right now," according to Jim Gillette, vice-president of IRN Inc. a consulting firm.[9]

3. To the extent other countries subsidize the production of raw materials such as steel and sell them at or below their cost of production, U.S. consumers and steel users everywhere benefit. Conversely, placing tariffs on steel is highly inflationary. According to some researchers, the new tariffs add about $9 billion to the cost of goods that are produced with steel—everything from toasters to minivans.[10]

4. Tariffs are often a disguised effort by the government to reward one group of citizens at the expense of another. According to a study by economists Joseph Francois and Laura Braghman of Trade Partnership Worldwide, tariffs cost anywhere from 7 to 14 jobs for

every job that is saved.[11] The problems of Big Steel have nothing to do with unfair trade; the term is simply used as a smokescreen for political purposes.

5. Protectionism makes domestic industries inefficient and consumers poorer. In the short term, it can provide temporary relief. But most of the low-cost rivals the big steel producers complain about are the mini-mills located in the U.S. These mills use less than one-third the labor of the large integrated mills, which allows them to be competitive with foreign producers. Other than the two largest U.S. producers, integrated steel makers not already in bankruptcy are likely to end up there with or without the tariffs.[12]

In the final analysis, most commentators believe Bush chose the votes of about 160,000 steel workers over the interests of American consumers, close foreign allies, poor developing nations and perhaps free trade itself. According to a *New York Times* article, former Treasury Secretary Paul O'Neill allegedly told a closed-door meeting of a foreign policy group that he disagreed with the decision of the administration and doubted that the move would save jobs. In his blunt style he held to the position that imposing tariffs jeopardizes our national interests as the world leader in promoting free trade.[13]

Europe, Japan, South Korea, Brazil, Norway, China and New Zealand all denounced the U.S. steel tariffs and filed complaints with the WTO. In November 2003, the tariffs were ruled to violate the GATT agreement. Faced with the threat of countervailing duties by countries across the globe, President Bush removed the steel tariffs in December 2003.[14] The net result of this attempt to protect a non-competitive industry is overwhelmingly negative. The union workers whose votes were courted won nothing in the long term and the false sense of security provided by the tariffs only postponed the changes needed in the U.S. steel industry, particularly plant modernization and labor costs.

Farming the Government

Begun in the dust bowls of the 1930s, farm relief was originally intended to aid marginal family farmers so they weren't driven to the poor house by unpredictable weather or gyrating commodity prices. Today nearly three-quarters of the money goes to the richest 10 percent of America's agricultural industry. Despite this giveaway, a farm bill was enacted in the U.S. in 2002 that obligates taxpayers to subsidize farmers to the tune of some $180 billion over the next decade. By some accounts, the final cost may be many times this figure. Even at $180 billion, the legislation is approximately 70 percent higher than the current subsidy program.[15]

These subsidies guarantee U.S. farmers minimum payments for their crops. By design, subsidies drive down the market price of farm commodities (except for those, like dairy products, that are kept artificially high by another agricultural policy known as price supports). As farm prices decline, higher subsidies are triggered and overproduction is accelerated. This chain of events is trade distorting and precisely counter to how free markets are meant to work. It also leads to surpluses that lower commodity prices to such a degree that poor developing countries are robbed of a chance to export their farm products. For decades Democratic and Republican administrations have lectured the world, and Europe in particular, on cutting agricultural subsidies and moving toward direct income payments to support their farmers. The U.S. government often does exactly the opposite of what it preaches.

At the end of 2001, Washington promised to discuss phasing out agricultural subsidies and improve the access of developing nations to agricultural exports. This pledge, made at the WTO meeting at Doha, convinced many developing countries that they could get a fair shake despite prior evidence that international rules were tilted in favor of wealthy nations. With passage of the 2002 farm bill suspicions rose and questions about further trade liberalization resurfaced.

During my trip to South Africa in November 2002, I heard repeated complaints about how farm subsidies in developed countries were derailing Africa's chance to export its way out of poverty.[16] Discussing the situation with South Africans representing a variety of views, I sensed a palpable feeling of disgust and desperation. They were offended by the conflicting rhetoric coming from countries in the Northern Hemisphere who extolled the virtues of free trade while practicing just the opposite. For instance, the 25,000 cotton growers in the United States are generally prosperous (average net worth $800,000) and correspondingly powerful. Therefore, the U.S. spends approximately $2 billion a year subsidizing inefficient, high-cost producers of cotton. According to a study published by the World Bank, the resulting glut of cotton costs African countries $250 million in lost sales annually. The policies followed by most developed countries to placate their farmers have proven exceedingly detrimental to many of the poorest countries and make hypocrites of those preaching the efficacy of free trade.[17] Particularly around elections, garnering a few more farm bloc votes proves hard for politicians to forego. Despite the harmful effects subsidies produce, principle gets thrown aside when political power is up for grabs. What is potentially most alarming, however, is that subsidies create the proverbial slippery slope that leads to tit-for-tat protectionism and puts the benefits of globalization at considerable risk.

Governing the Farm

Politicians worldwide have long accepted the need to subsidize farming—everyone needs to eat, the weather is volatile and farmers vote—enough said. But not only is political opinion often wrong, so too is conventional wisdom. There may be no better way to make this point than to examine the situation in New Zealand. New Zealand's economy is extremely dependent on farming. Calculated according to either output or employment, farming is roughly five times as important to New Zealand as it is to the United States. In 1984 subsidies to farmers consisted of 30 separate payments and export incentives and accounted for more than 30 percent of the production value of the entire industry. So when New Zealand's government decided to end almost all farm subsidies dramatically, politicians took a huge risk. But a drastic solution was needed as New Zealand's agricultural industry faced the same self-inflicted problems found in the U.S.—inflated real estate prices, environmental defilement and price-stifling overproduction.

Government support ended swiftly and completely with one time "exit grants" to farmers wanting to find other types of work once subsidies ended. As might be expected, the plan was rigorously resisted by those affected and the government was prepared to see 10 percent of its farmers fail. Despite dire predictions, farming in New Zealand adjusted to the transition and has never been healthier. The trade group, Federated Farmers of New Zealand, found the changes to be extremely positive to the agricultural industry. Although reform initially depressed land prices, within a decade they had rebounded and remain strong today. Contrary to earlier prognostications, only 1 percent of farms went out of business. Farm output, in constant dollars, has risen since the mid-1980s. And agriculture's share of economic output has also risen. Moreover, farm productivity has averaged 6 percent per annum since the elimination of subsidies versus 1 percent in the pre-reform period. To the astonishment of many, New Zealand farmers are able to compete successfully in world markets despite facing subsidies in most other countries.

Data from the Organization for Economic Cooperation and Development (OECD) show that agricultural subsidies (primarily in the form of scientific research) account for just 1 percent of the value of agricultural production in New Zealand whereas they represent 22 percent of the value of U.S. farm production. This means that New Zealand has the lowest level of subsidized farming among industrialized nations. These results are compelling and provide vivid evidence of how innovative and resourceful people can be in the absence of government interference. New Zealand farmers, required to adjust to new realities, reduced costs, created non-farm income opportunities and changed their production levels to correspond to market forces. Since farm industry suppliers could no longer rely on subsidies to inflate demand, the cost of supplies fell benefiting farmers and consumers alike. Finally, marginal land that was farmed solely because of lucrative subsidies was converted to other purposes while fertilizer subsidies, and the consequent overuse, ended. Needless to say, the environment benefited enormously.[18]

As the New Zealand farm example vividly illustrates, unconventional political thinking can achieve surprisingly positive results. Eliminate subsidies and you create a more competitive, prosperous farming industry—how heretical. So why do governments around the world do just the opposite? Why isn't there more long-term thinking that places the common good ahead of special interests? Changes—even good ones—are likely to affect some group adversely before the benefits to the majority become obvious. Without steel tariffs or farm subsidies some jobs will be lost. The fact that these jobs may be lost anyway is of little consolation to the affected wage earners or their representatives.

The importance people place on keeping their jobs and maintaining their standard of living is understandable and certainly can't be disregarded. Preserving the status quo always seems preferable and the uncertainty of new developments is a challenge most people would rather avoid. The reality, however, is that change is an inevitable fact of life and changing conditions necessitate making adjustments. Those individuals who made a living in the horse, saddle or carriage business struggled mightily when the automobile gained popularity. Eventually they adjusted by learning new skills or finding better ways to use what expertise they already possessed. Technological improvements and globalization will lead to "lost jobs" somewhere. Those forced to make changes in their work or residency may need temporary assistance from government and/or private sources. In the long run more jobs (often better paying and more satisfying) are created than lost in the expansion of global trade.[19]

Getting Up and Moving On

Solving the transitional problems that inevitably arise as global commerce expands requires honesty, education and engagement. Government leaders must frankly tell the electorate that there will be winners and losers as protectionist measures are eliminated and new markets are opened. Citizens of developing countries fear that the rich developed countries will take advantage of them and capture all the benefits of globalization. Yet economists throughout the world are virtually unanimous in their belief that freer trade has significantly reduced worldwide poverty. A study by the London-based Center for Economic Research states that the number of truly poor people was more than halved between 1950 and 1992 and this positive trend has continued.[20] The truth is that jobs will be lost and factories will move because of liberalized trade. But expanded trade, coupled with adequate environmental safeguards, will ultimately improve the well-being of the nation—both economically and socially.

Those who face dislocations need to be given assistance. The government can use the higher tax revenue generated from increased economic growth to provide a safety net in the form of retraining opportunities and temporary transition payments to those adversely affected. Business and political leaders must educate their constituents about the benefits and costs involved. The positives should not be exaggerated nor the negatives denied; improving the economic literacy of all citizens is the best way to get politicians to make good economic decisions. Finally, the electorate must be engaged in a way that builds coalitions for long-term oriented policies and that puts the economic needs of the majority ahead of narrowly based special interests. PoliticalShortimers, preoccupied with winning the next election, will refuse to make short-term sacrifices or take controversial positions until enough of the electorate demands action.

Educating and engaging citizens on the benefits of liberalized trade may require time and effort but the arguments aren't difficult. Trade devoid of tariffs, subsidies, quotas or any other form of nationalistic favoritism results in more choices and lower prices for businesses and consumers. Free trade fosters vigorous competition that encourages greater productivity and innovation. Benefits similar to those New Zealand experienced become evident soon after a nation removes trade barriers. But the benefits of liberalized trade go beyond economic efficiency; the freedom to trade is a basic human right and a prerequisite for true political freedom. Countries with open economic systems provide more opportunities for their citizens to prosper and encourage peaceful cooperation with their neighbors.

Looking Back—Peeking Forward

In section two, chapters 3, 4 and 5 have examined how prominent members of four groups actively involved in the globalization process define and pursue their self-interest. Business leaders often make the owners of the company their top priority. Since management usually owns a significant amount of stock, their *ME*-oriented focus is understandable but shortsighted. Environmentalists make the interdependence of all living things their mantra and in so doing have a focus on *US*. Politicians concentrate on winning the next election while labor leaders are intent on improving job security for their members. Both of these groups do what they can to get the approval of their respective electorates; i.e., *THEM*. Obviously all these groups have competing considerations and constituencies and disruptive conflicts often result. Before examining ways to mitigate or solve the conflicts, a few more perspectives must be considered.

The first three chapters of section two have been presented from the vantage point of economically developed countries. Developing countries have a somewhat different point of view and often have needs and desires that diverge from those of richer, more technologically advanced regions of the world. The next two chapters, therefore, look at how the leaders of two developing countries, South Africa and Argentina, have approached economic integration. We will also look at a somewhat unique country, Singapore, as its global economic success provides valuable, if somewhat qualified, lessons. These three countries provide useful examples of *ME*, *THEM* and *US* governing orientations that have indelibly affected their respective societies.

Notes

[1] "What Next for Jacques Chirac and His Dominant Centre-Right?" *The Economist*, 22 June 2002, 45.

[2] "A World Driven by Trade," *Investor's Business Daily*, 13 February 2004, A14.

[3] Paul Bluestein, "New Faith in Free Trade: in Break with Allies, Oxfam Backs Globalization," *The Washington Post*, 11 April 2002, E1.

[4] James Gwartney and Robert Lawson, *Economic Freedom of the World: 2002 Annual Report*, (Vancouver, BC: The Fraser Institute, 2002).

[5] "The World Trade Organization In Brief," *http://www.wto.org/ english/thewto_e/whatis_e/inbrief_e/inbr00_e.htm*: 8 July 2002.

6 "World Subsidies to Support Over-Fishing are a Quarter of the Value of Fish Trade," *Progressive Policy Institute Trade Fact of the Week, www. ppionline.com*: 15 May 2002.

7 Edward Gresser, "America's Hidden Tax on the Poor; The Case for Reforming U.S. Tariff Policy," *Progressive Policy Institute Policy Report* (Washington), March 2002, 6–7.

8 David Ignatius, "So Much for Free Trade," *The Washington Post*, 8 March 2002, A33.

9 "Honda Airlifts Japanese Steel to North American Plants," *Bloomberg News: Business & Finance,* messenger@ecm.bloomberg.com: 9 July 2002.

10 Andrew Cassel, "A Hardhearted Approach to Solving Big Steel's Troubles," *The Philadelphia Inquirer*, 18 March 2002.

11 "Man of Steel?" *The Wall Street Journal*, 4 March 2002, A14.

12 "Rust Never Sleeps," *The Economist*, 9 March 2002, 62.

13 Joseph Kahn and Richard W. Stevenson, "Treasury Official Is Said to Fault Steel Tariff Move," *The New York Times*, 16 March 2002.

14 Stephen Hall, "Controversies Over the WTO," *A World Connected, http://www.aworldconnedted.org/article.php?od=623&print=1*: 24 March 2004.

15 Andrew Cassel, "Why U.S. Farm Subsidies are Bad for the World," *The Philadelphia Inquirer*, 6 May 2002.

16 Nicholas D. Kristof, "Farm Subsidies That Kill," *The New York Times*, 5 July 2002.

17 Ibid.

18 Chris Edwards and Tad DeHaven, "Save the Farms—End the Subsidies," *The Washington Post*, 3 March 2002, B7.

19 David Isaac, "Sowell Sees Politics to Blame for Failed Economic Policies," *Investor's Business Daily*, 7 June 2002, A16.

20 Jeremy Gaunt, "Globalization Has Helped Poor, Study Says," *Yahoo! News, http://dailynews.yahoo.com*: 8 July 2002.

Chapter Six

Two Countries — Two Cultures

BlameGamers

We have previously looked at the problems created by Enron and other self-serving EntreprenurCelebs. Now, let's consider Argentina. What does Argentina have in common with Enron? In the 90s both were considered economic superstars—hailed by all and widely emulated. By the next decade, both were bankrupt. Enron's board of directors blamed everyone from its accountants to its senior executives; Argentina's government pointed fingers at everyone from Investor Vigilantes to its neighbors in both hemispheres. Employees, shareholders and citizens suffered enormously; those actually responsible looked for scapegoats. Argentina is a country that, for the better part of a century, has experienced periodic economic turmoil and social unrest. What finally broke the back of the country? And, more importantly, what is being done to stabilize the economy so that Argentina can re-enter the global economy and enjoy the benefits of sustainable economic growth?

A Brief History of Turbulence

Early in the 20th century, Argentina's grain-based economy was considered the breadbasket of the world. To be "rich as an Argentine" was a dream of most Latin Americans. Even today, Argentina has a wealth of natural resources with its fertile plains growing enough grain to feed its 37 million people many times over. In the 1940s, however, General Juan Peron declared war on the "rich" with a combination of populist policies, nationalism and extravagant patronage. These policies continued for much of the bloody military dictatorships in the 1970s and 1980s. Nonetheless, Argentines stuck to the belief that they had more in common with southern Europe than their South American neighbors. Toward the end of the 20th century—after more than 50 years of excessive government spending, counterproductive economic policies, large public sector deficits, recurring bouts of hyperinflation, and a bloated, corrupt patronage system—Argentina's economy was in critical condition.

On July 9, 1989 Carlos Menem became President of Argentina, representing the first peaceful transfer from one democratically elected president to another since 1928. The new president became the leader of a country that was impoverished, its national currency was in shambles and wages were insufficient for most citizens to obtain basic necessities. As a result, increasing social violence made it extremely difficult to govern or maintain order. The solution, according to conventional wisdom, was to open Argentina's economy, permitting it to participate in expanding global trade. Many important changes would be required: curbing inflation and deficits, privatizing state owned businesses and significantly reducing protectionist policies. In 1991 President Menem took the decisive step of pegging the Argentine peso one-to-one to the U.S. dollar. This "Convertibility Law" proved very effective in curbing inflation. Over a period of several years many state owned businesses—airlines, railroads, power plants, telephone, postal and water systems, steel mills and coal mines—were transferred to the private sector.[1] Labor unions might have been expected to oppose privatization. They were, however, offered enticements: participation in the management of a variety of new companies. The union leadership stood to benefit handsomely and, therefore, bestowed their blessings on the reform. These measures, coupled with favorable international economic conditions and a spurt in tax collections reflecting the income received from the privatizations, led to a prosperous economy into the early 90s.

Eliminating, or even moderating, protectionist policies was a much more difficult assignment. Businesses and unions who prospered from state subsidies designed to protect domestic industries against foreign competition were loath to give up their extravagant benefits. And so, while major corporations participated in government policy deliberations, they offered only superficial support. Their investment decisions continued to be based on their short-term interests with little consideration given to the long-term consequences for the country.[2]

Pegging the peso to the dollar did subdue inflation. But with an overvalued peso tied to a rising dollar, Argentina's exports were disadvantaged, severely restricting the ability of the country to participate in international trade. The government returned to its practice of subsidizing exporters thus generating higher federal deficits. These deficits were partially offset by the foreign investments made by IVs who became enamored with Argentina once they saw that the peso would not be devalued. Financiers were generally not concerned with the long-term economic health of Argentina; maximizing their short-term investment returns was almost always paramount. In pursuit of those returns, they move their money around the world at the drop of a hat. The government, understanding that IVs provided the funds needed to finance the deficits, relaxed fiscal restraint and effectively relinquished control over domestic economic policy.[3]

In the political arena, corruption and lavish spending were rampant. Argentina's 24 provinces collect virtually no taxes. Rather, governors of each province receive money from the central government and spend it as they choose, often on swollen payrolls and political patronage. According to Joseph Tulchin, director of the Latin American program at the Woodrow Wilson International Center for Scholars in Washington, D.C., "No one controls the spending. The states can spend the federal government into bankruptcy."[4]

Government officials who surrounded President Menem had access to inside information about reforms and privatizations and used it to influence policies and gain maximum personal advantage. Bribes and kickbacks were used to wear down opponents and reward confidants. Trade union official Luis Barrionuevo declared, "Nobody makes money by working." To solve these problems he proposed, "Everyone stop stealing for 2 years."[5] Even the Buenos Aires provincial police were implicated in a variety of illegal actions: auto theft, drug trafficking and prostitution. The quest for money and power became a prime motivator and corruption penetrated all public institutions.[6]

By the end of the 1990s, as Menem's term was coming to an end, Argentina lapsed into a harsh recession. The Convertibility Law had eventually made it impossible for Argentina to compete globally as the costs of its goods were extraordinarily high when measured in U.S. dollars. Exports continued to decline and deficits expanded. Money from privatizations had long since dried up and IVs, increasingly skittish after the economic collapse of Russia and assorted financial debacles in other parts of the world, pulled the plug on new investments. Foreign debt, totaling some $160 billion had doubled since 1994 and could not be serviced.[7] The government was concerned about the rising incidence of social discontent and solicited the cooperation of union leaders who had enjoyed some success in handling these problems. Many leaders were party to the corruption within their ranks and demanded that the government permit them to maintain control over assorted discretionary funds. In meeting these demands, the government relinquished any opportunity to introduce more ethical behavior into the political system. The governors of the provinces, often members of family dynasties, insisted on receiving their traditionally high level of government distributions despite the dwindling level of national taxes. A good portion of these funds was, in turn, earmarked for those who could deliver political favors.[8]

It should be no surprise, then, that the Argentine society became increasingly polarized. The middle class saw its standard of living decline precipitously while a small group of politically connected citizens flaunted their wealth shamelessly. Social inequities became more obvious and extreme. "...the middle class has lost the ability to plan for its future and that of its children. Foresight—one of its classic attributes—gave way to a 'live it for the day' attitude, to taking advantage of whatever opportunities might arise: a trip abroad or the purchase of upscale household appliances."[9] The largely egalitarian society of the past was now sharply divided and disconnected.

Fernando de la Rúa became president of Argentina in December 1999. A conservative member of the upstart Alianza para la Justica, el Trabajo, y la Educacion coalition, he had to govern with the opposition of the liberal Peronists. This made the implementation of badly needed reforms a daunting challenge. De la Rúa inherited an economy in crisis with high unemployment and rising social unrest. The country was ready to explode.

According to Luis Alberto Romero's excellent book, *A History of Argentina in the Twentieth Century,* de la Rúa was an ineffective leader. He was a petty negotiator, mistrusted his collaborators, was a poor delegator of responsibilities and had difficulty making decisions. He was surrounded by a group of young advisors, headed by his son, whose prime focus was to strengthen de la Rúa's image as a leader. Loyalty rather than talent was the primary criterion used in determining the hierarchy within the government.[10]

A Revealing Experience

In February 2000 my son, Eric, traveled to Argentina in conjunction with a Business Development Mission of the U.S. Department of Commerce. During that trip, he had occasion to witness some of de la Rúa's preoccupation with his image. He later told me:

> *The most difficult assignment I had was putting together the meeting Secretary of Commerce William Daley would have at* Casa Rosada *with President de la Rúa. The two principals were to have a meeting followed by a press conference at which they would sign a Joint Statement on E-Commerce Cooperation and launch a new web site to encourage trade between U.S. and Argentine small and medium-sized businesses (SMEs). Every minute a new wrinkle emerged to complicate matters: the President decided not to participate in the press conference, then he did; the Joint Statement wasn't fully negotiated; the launch of the internet site "wasn't Presidential", etc. Eventually all of the problems, except for the Joint Statement, which we were negotiating up*

to the last moment, were resolved. The Joint Statement was never signed —in its place the principals voiced their support for "continued cooperation in the field of E-Commerce." The most difficult part of the press conference was the launch of the Internet site. In reality, the site would go online from the server at the American Embassy, but we wanted the Secretary and the President to launch it symbolically at Casa Rosada. *We rigged up a fake mouse for the two principals to push; at the same time someone in the back of the room would turn on a projector which would project a simulated image of the website. To anyone watching, it would be fairly dramatic and look like the two principals had done something to bring the site on-line (sort of a high-tech ribbon cutting). The Argentine government officials didn't understand the smoke and mirrors and didn't see a need for all the glitz and "politics". But we insisted and finally the Argentines agreed that Secretary Daley could do it, while President de la Rúa would just watch. I really don't know how much should be read into this reluctance, but it seemed clear that the President's staff wanted to create an appearance of regality around de la Rúa and had no time for American showmanship. As U.S. government officials we were used to glitz; in this situation we knew it didn't matter how the site appeared to be launched as long as it ultimately went online.*

Throughout the day at Casa Rosada, *I got the impression that the Argentines were trying hard to create an imperial facade and didn't want to diminish the President's image even if the substance of it was unaffected. While one can argue that President Clinton's or Bush's staffs would have similar concerns, I believe that, for the most part, decisions like these made at the White*

*House are made based first on substance, second on
image. In hindsight, de la Rúa's preoccupation with his
image looks like Nero fiddling while Rome burned.*

Patron, Disciplinarian or Enabler

With private financing drying up, Argentina turned once
again to the International Monetary Fund where it had
received periodic financial bailouts for many years. A very
brief history of this controversial institution will help put the
IMF-Argentina saga in perspective. In 1944, at the UN
Monetary and Financial Conference at Bretton Woods, New
Hampshire, the IMF was assigned the task of preventing economic catastrophes such as the Great Depression. A few
decades later, the mission of the IMF shifted as it became
increasingly enmeshed in unraveling the debt problems of
developing countries. Unfortunately, the debt dilemmas of
many of these countries have turned out to be of the chronic
variety. In the 1980s the IMF began attaching one-size-fits-
all, free market reform conditions to the countries receiving
its largesse. In other words, to get the loans these governments had to agree to market-opening trade liberalization
policies regardless of the strength or maturity of their institutions or industries.

Critics from the left argue that most of the distressed
economies receiving IMF aid don't have the financial infrastructure or sophistication to regulate a market economy
effectively. As a result, loans to these countries further exaggerate the already wide gap between rich and poor. The rich
have the contacts and knowledge to siphon off most of the
newly flowing money while little if any of the money trick-
les down to the poor. Despite the best intentions, the over-
indebted country has little to show for the rescue effort.
Critics from the right find the top-down economic planning

model of the IMF equally objectionable, as command and control tactics are an anathema to free market doctrine. Of course, even if IMF policy prescriptions are wise, there is no incentive to follow the rules once the money has been received; the IMF has a history of continuing to dole out loans even if the country in question fails to comply with IMF prescriptions.[11] Argentina is a prime example of the IMF continuing to lend money to a country despite its inability and/or refusal to conform to the agency's funding requirements. As a result, outstanding IMF loans to Argentina amount to an imprudently high 15 percent of agency totals.[12]

Back to Unreality

The Alianza's unraveling began in earnest with a well-publicized Senate scandal. Argentina had promised the IMF it would enact a labor reform package to increase competitiveness and efficiency. It had little business support and considerable union resistance. To smooth passage of the bill the government first threatened to cut union funding and then secretly negotiated to provide covert support. While this maneuver enabled the law to pass in the Chamber of Deputies, Senators were determined to show their independence and restore the under-the-table reward system that had worked so well under President Menem. When the government finally decided to provide the compensation desired by the Senators, the bill was passed. When a well-respected journalist exposed this sleazy maneuver, Vice President Alvarez, in his role as head of the Senate, denounced the corruption. Unfortunately, neither his party nor the opposition nor any government officials came to his support. In fact, the President actually rewarded the guilty party with a promotion. Trapped by his uncompromising stance, Alvarez resigned the Vice Presidency. His resignation made clear that one of the major planks in Alianza's electoral platform—that of introducing ethical behavior to the Argentine political process—was now forsaken. The Alianza coalition was in disarray and was never able to recover.[13]

On December 20, 2001 a large segment of the Buenos Aires middle class flooded the streets with their pots and pans in hand to protest the freezing of their bank deposits and life savings which the government imposed to prevent the collapse of Argentina's economy. Protests by the poor and unemployed were commonplace; protests by the middle class were something new and unanticipated. After making a futile call for a government of national unity, President de la Rúa presented his resignation and unceremoniously left the presidential palace in a helicopter.[14]

Who's in Charge?

In rapid-fire succession, three prominent politicians occupied and then vacated Argentina's presidency. On January 2, 2002 Eduardo Duhalde became the fourth politician in two weeks to assume Argentina's presidency. A member of Menem's populist Peronist Party, Duhalde inherited a rudderless and virtually penniless country. According to government statistics, over 11,000 Argentines fell into poverty daily (earning less than $3 a day). The rapidly disappearing middle class turned in droves to pawnshops to sell their valued possessions. Grocery stores raised their prices despite the historic decline in earning power. A 70 percent devaluation in the peso forced prices up and real wages down. Although local products such as flour and canned tomatoes had minimal real increases in production costs, their prices surged 166 percent and 118 percent respectively. Prior to 1999, Argentina's per capita income was just under $9,000—double Mexico's and three times that of Poland. By mid-2002 Argentina's per capita income was on a par with Jamaica and Belarus at approximately $2,500. More than one-fifth of

Argentines were unemployed and more than half lived below the official poverty line.[15]

Duhalde faced Herculean obstacles; not the least of which was the impending Presidential election. No politician wants to make tough decisions that offend labor unions and other key constituencies, particularly near new elections. The first priority of the Duhalde government became that of appeasing the IMF so that additional funds could be secured. In an attempt to achieve some IMF preconditions for a rescue package, Argentina's three largest provinces agreed to cut their deficits and stop issuing private quasi-currencies. In addition, an economic subversion law, used to persecute foreign bankers, was repealed. Nonetheless, a comprehensive and coherent economic plan that would address all of Argentina's problems, including a dismantling of the patronage system, was left unaddressed. In the absence of such a plan, the crisis in Argentina intensified and the risk of contagion to other Latin American countries increased.[16]

What's the Point?

Finger pointing has become a national obsession in Argentina. The parties most faulted for their dire economic and social conditions are the IMF, international bankers and local and national politicians. A dispassionate examination of the influential groups who are currently being blamed is essential to determining their culpability. It also leads to what some may think are surprising conclusions.

Those who fault the IMF, and there are many, cite the harsh and insensitive pressure on Argentina to reduce its deficits and establish greater fiscal discipline since such actions led to financial hardships for many Argentines. The fact that the IMF has indulged Argentina for decades and never really enforced its "austere" conditions on the government does little to blunt the criticism. Neither does the fact that many observers blame the IMF for being too soft on Argentina and letting its government persist in its ill-conceived policies. In 2003 the IMF issued a report examining the failure to sound the alarm about the untenable peso-dollar peg and its excessive borrowing. It must be remembered that Argentina solicited help from the IMF when free-spending populist programs and extravagant patronage spawned unsupportable debts. When the conditions imposed by the much-maligned IMF are too lenient and the borrowing country fails to stabilize, member governments and, ultimately, taxpayers around the world pick up the tab. Balance this against the risk of political instability if financial support is withheld for fear the loans won't be repaid. It is easy to see why the IMF has had a difficult time deciding between tolerance and stringency with debtor nations.

Foreign commercial banks have taken their share of criticism, particularly from Argentine citizens. "I'll never put my money in a bank again. I'm a victim of a fraud performed by a selected group of first-line banking corporations and the state." So said Daniel Muzio, an Argentine photo editor who invested his 20-year savings in Citibank, Bank of Boston and Metropolitan Life Insurance Company. As a result of the government freezing bank withdrawals in 2002, Muzio believes his $160,000 in retirement and college education savings may be lost. Even if he is wrong, the money has already lost about two-thirds of its value as a result of the devaluation of the peso.[17] Foreign bank participation is considered an important symbol of financial viability for an emerging market economy and, over the past decade, foreign-owned banks were encouraged to become major participants in the Argentine banking system. These banks bet on the maintenance of a strong, sound economy based, in part, on Argentina's robust economic growth of the early 1990s. But recent government policies have favored domestic depositors over the largely foreign-owned banks, since the latter are an easy scapegoat. The banks, which will likely lose billions of dollars before stability is restored, can be accused of imprudence on several fronts, but they are not the primary architects of Argentina's current chaos.

Other IVs, particularly investment bankers and brokers, have also been accused of sabotaging Argentina's economy. It is true that, in the latter half of the nineties, as emerging markets around the globe deteriorated and Argentina's ability to service its debt became suspect, financiers used their computers, cell phones and fax machines to move funds to safer, more predictable investments. These actions exacerbated Argentina's plight; interest rates skyrocketed when IVs moved their money to safer soil and there were few investors to take up the slack. Banks and brokers did not, however, cause Argentina's problems. They were simply acting in their perceived self-interest by refusing to continue investments in a country whose financial situation was rapidly deteriorating.

Have Ideas Will Relocate

Just as investors will move their capital out of insecure and unaccommodating parts of the world, entrepreneurs will make tracks for countries that appreciate and protect their job-producing efforts. Argentina's outmoded and ineffective trade, labor and property laws are antagonistic to entrepreneurship; its regulatory framework protects the status quo, anathema to innovators. Many Argentine entrepreneurs are, therefore, fleeing their country for Europe and North America. Indicative of their ingenuity, many Argentines took advantage of a special visa class granted to foreign executives who establish a branch of a home-country business in the United States. This visa, called an L1, is a stepping-stone to a green card and permanent residency. Daryl Buffenstein, general counsel of the American Immigration Lawyers Association, believes, "This visa is the most important visa for economic development for the United States. It creates employment and brings money. The sad thing is that another country's loss could be our gain."[18] In this case, it is Argentina's loss due to regulations that encourage not only capital flight but brain drain as well.

Zeroing in on the Culprits

While the IMF and most bankers can find ways to rationalize their actions, Argentina's politicians have few defenses or supporters. Not only were many economic policies counter-productive, but many government officials were, to one degree or another, enmeshed in corrupt practices. While the national government did make an effort to control spending, provincial governments continued to gorge themselves. Government spending as a percent of gross domestic product climbed precipitously. Government efforts to implement even minimal reforms were laudable but failed because they were not backed by a long-term commitment. As a result, The 2004 World Competitiveness Survey rankings compiled by the Institute for Management Development of Lausanne, Switzerland, ranked Argentina 59th out of the 60 countries examined.[19]

Foreign business people identify corruption as a significant factor inhibiting trade and investment. In Argentina corruption charges are difficult to prosecute and convictions rare because the judicial system is cumbersome and ineffective and plea-bargaining is not allowed.[20] The situation was perhaps best described by Uruguay's President Jorge Batlle when he called his Argentine neighbors "a bunch of thieves, from top to bottom."[21]

Reflections in the Mirror

There is more than enough blame to go around. To varying degrees, government officials, the IMF and a multitude of financial institutions have all put their narrow self-interest ahead of Argentina's long-term interests. While the ME-focused responses of these three groups did exacerbate a difficult situation, the primary responsibility for Argentina's sorry state of affairs must be laid at the doorstep of the citizens. Rosendo Fraga, a political analyst, made this diagnosis: "We are like one of those old, rich families, where the grandfather made a fortune, the son began to spend it, and the grandson finished it off."[22]

History shows that even despots can be removed from power when people become sufficiently dissatisfied with their living conditions. The fact that Argentina is a democracy, albeit fledgling, requires that its citizens insist, through the ballot box and other peaceful means, that those leading the country act honestly, responsibly and effectively or be replaced by ones that will. Yet they, like most of us, have been guilty of closing their eyes to dishonest behavior and incompetent leadership for far too long. All choices have consequences—Argentina's are extremely distasteful. The citizens of Argentina stood idly by as their country lived beyond its means and built up an unsupportable amount of debt. Now they must pay the price of that irresponsible behavior. Those same citizens believed for decades that everyone else was to blame for the problems they suffered. They see needed reforms as being thrust upon them by foreigners and, therefore, evade or renounce them at the first opportunity. The key to meaningful reform is for citizens to recognize that changing the policies of their economic and political institutions serves their best interest.

In this regard, Eric had an interesting and insightful encounter. Even though impressed by Argentina's beef, wine and women, he remembered some comments made to him by an Argentine woman who worked at the U.S. Ambassador's residence.

I was working with her putting together a reception at the residence for the Secretary of Commerce and the U.S. business community. After the reception, which was quite successful, I thanked her for her help and complimented her about the wonderful Argentine culture. I told her I could get into a lifestyle where one takes a siesta in the afternoon and has late, leisurely dinners of beef and wine every night. She told me that it was not all it was cracked up to be and that Argentina's economy was suffering. I said that I didn't see it and that everywhere I looked I saw activity and packed stores. She told me that she would much rather Argentina adopt a more conscientious work ethic and, while she didn't use exactly those terms, she conveyed the strong impression that she considered her countrymen a little lazy and decadent. Although there are other Latin cultures that have similar approaches to the day and aren't bankrupt, I got the impression she may have been alerting me to some emerging fault lines in Argentina's otherwise beautiful facade.

A New Beginning

On May 25, 2003 Nestor Kirchner took office as Argentina's new president. A former governor of the sparsely populated Patagonia province, he is, by many accounts, a pragmatic populist. Under Mr. Kirchner Argentina's economy has bounced back smartly. The surprisingly quick recovery has been aided by abundant idle capacity and soaring prices for farm exports. Unfortunately, neither of these fortuitous conditions will last forever. New investment is badly needed, but is hindered by Argentina's disregard for the rule of law, its unwieldy court system and its onerous indebtedness. According to Manuel Mora y Araujo, a sociologist and pollster, "People think the law should be respected but nobody does respect it. Those who steal a lot are seen as corrupt, but people think it's OK to steal a little."[23] And according to a local analyst, "Argentina is a country that has always lived through these great boom and bust cycles. The problem is that when the economy starts to boom, it seems everyone starts to suffer from amnesia about the bust."[24] On a more positive note, Anoop Singh, IMF chief for the western hemisphere, is cautiously optimistic about the debt burden, "I don't think the Argentine population will tolerate high fiscal deficits and inflation any more. There may have been a culture shift."[25] There is no doubt Argentines are resilient and resourceful people; with hard work and the assumption of greater personal responsibility conditions are likely to continue improving.

DisciplineSlingers

Singapore, home of the exotic Singapore Sling cocktail, stands in sharp contrast to Argentina. This tiny country (647 square kilometers) has developed a vibrant economy that has skillfully integrated into the global marketplace. Unlike Argentina, Singapore is largely devoid of even the most basic resources, including fresh water. This has led, in part, to the development of one of the most liberal trading regimes in the world; more than 99 percent of all imports enter Singapore duty-free. Its per capita income, at over $28,000, is one of the highest in the world. The government-owned Singapore Airlines is consistently rated one of the best in the world and its port is one of the busiest.

In absolute terms, and especially when compared to Argentina's volatile political and economic landscape, Singapore is an extremely stable country. Singapore ranked 2nd in the 2004 Index of Economic Freedom, 114 places ahead of Argentina.[26] Whereas Argentina placed 49th (second worst) in the 2004 World Competitiveness Survey, Singapore was near the top at number two.[27] Given its high rankings in both these categories, it should be no surprise that Singapore has been ranked the number one business environment in the Asia Pacific region.[28]

How Do They Do It?

Singapore is, in many respects, unique. Its size, history and location coupled with the emphasis put on strategic thinking and instilling a distinct set of values can't be found anywhere else in the world. While in Singapore, I met with Tommy Koh, Harvard educated lawyer, Singapore's former Ambassador to the UN and U.S., senior advisor to the government and head of the Institute of Policy Studies.[29] I asked him if he thought Singapore's successful economic model could be replicated elsewhere. He quickly responded in the affirmative. Specifically, Ambassador Koh cited numerous aspects of Singapore's ingrained system of values that were not a function of geography and could be replicated elsewhere. First, and perhaps most important, is how realism, pragmatism and adaptability are applied toward achieving the goals and objectives of the country. If an idea doesn't initially work, Singaporeans are willing and able to change direction quickly. Second, citizens have learned to accept a long-term view and look for what serves the collective good. Bureaucratic turf battles, which waste time and energy, are rare. Education is highly prized as is saving money for the next generation (Singaporeans are reported to save over 40 percent of their income). Last, but far from least, Singapore's citizens are disciplined, honest and exhibit a high level of integrity. As Koh Buck Song, head of marketing communications for Singapore's Economic Development Board, succinctly put it, "In Singapore, there is a culture that is anti-corruption."[30] Because of this, the government is widely viewed as squeaky clean.

Corrupt Me at My Peril

Berlin-based Transparency International (TI) surveyed 133 countries for its 2003 "Corruption Perception Index" (CPI).

CPI, which is based on 17 surveys of 13 independent insti-tutions, reflects perceived levels of corruption among politi-cians and public officials. Singapore placed 5th in TI's rank-ing system and is one of a very few countries that scored 9 (10 is the maximum) or higher. Argentina, where corruption is perceived as being rampant, had a score of 2.5, ranking 92nd out of 133.[31]

Companies that yield to bribery face significant risks and additional costs in the current ultra-competitive global econ-omy. Bribery, illegal in most countries, takes place behind closed doors where those involved spend substantial time and resources to keep their actions secret. Relationships built on corrupt practices are necessarily unhealthy, unstable and unenforceable. Eventually, bribes are likely to become public knowledge: reputations are lost and perpetrators prosecuted. From the perspective of international trade, bribery presents many additional pitfalls. First, bribery degrades markets by misallocating resources; those who gain business through bribes are unlikely to be the lowest cost and/or highest qual-ity producers. (If they were, they would not have to resort to bribes.) Taxpayers and consumers are, therefore, saddled with more costly or inferior goods and services. In countries where corruption is endemic, people do not trust the government and develop their own, more expensive mechanisms for resolving disputes or enforcing contracts. According to Philip M. Nichols, legal studies professor at the University of Pennsylvania, "money goes to supporting the government system and money goes to supporting the shadow system; twice as much money goes to bureaucracies as it should. That means money is not going to increasing food production, or to health, or to enlarging the economy."[32] It is worth noting that, based on TI's work, the most corrupt countries are also the most impoverished.

Finally, numerous commentators have found a close cor-relation between high levels of corruption and low levels of foreign investment. According to Nichols there are several reasons for this finding. Corruption increases the time wasted on bureaucratic in-fighting, information is harder and more expensive to acquire, relationships are more tenuous and contracts less enforceable. Most importantly, most people find unethical and illegal behavior demeaning and distasteful.[33] Clearly Argentina is one of many countries that could learn from Singapore's very successful formula for attaining corruption-free economic integration and growth.

No One is Perfect

No country is perfect either. It is not surprising, therefore, that the media has described Singapore in both complimentary and critical terms. Many commentators view Singapore's political oversight as unnecessarily strict. While in recent years Singapore has become a more open society with more tolerant government regulation, restrictions remain on the right to speak freely or publish without censorship.[34] In August 2002, for example, *Bloomberg News* published an article about the appointment of Ho Ching as executive director of Temasek, the domestic investment arm of the Singapore government. She is the wife of the Deputy Prime Minister and daughter-in-law of senior minister Lee Kuan Yew. A number of Singaporean leaders felt that the article implied nepotism was involved. Three officials threatened legal proceedings and Bloomberg issued an apology, agreed to pay unspecified damages and costs and promised not to make similar allegations in the future. Singapore's leaders claim that restrictions on the media are necessary to maintain the discipline and stability that has made Singapore an economic powerhouse.[35]

Restrictions extend to some pretty mundane areas of everyday life. A tee shirt I bought in a downtown mall said it most pointedly, "Singapore is a fine city." "Fine" referring to the financial penalties for everything from spitting to flower picking and more draconian measures for what are viewed as more offensive transgressions. In a constructive vein, the country offers numerous awards to its citizens to encourage desired behaviors such as courtesy and kindness. The Economic Development Board sponsors the Phoenix award to recognize entrepreneurs who, after having failed, have gone on to achieve success. The purpose of this award is to allay the stigma often attached to business failures and bankruptcies and to encourage entrepreneurs not to give up. These are just a few of the examples of specific rewards and punishments used by the government to motivate Singaporeans' behavior.

Years of these carrot and stick policies have engendered a very disciplined culture amongst Singaporeans. They seem willing to forego some personal flexibility and freedom for the benefits that come from a cohesive, vibrant economy. An example—two teenage boys stood with me and my wife on a paved island in the middle of a street that was no more than 30 feet wide from sidewalk to sidewalk. The light was red but there was no traffic coming in either direction as far as the eye could see. Teenagers in most other countries would have crossed the street, against the light, without thinking twice. These two stood for what appeared to be a very long time waiting patiently for the light to change. What self-restraint! We also watched with some amazement as a large crowd of people quietly waited in line for their turn to enter a popular department store. In other countries we have visited the scene at the entrance to a very busy store is usually just shy of chaotic. Following the rules to the letter has been so internalized in Singapore that people seem to accept restrictions without objection.

This passive acceptance of whatever rules the government promulgates may not, however, last forever. A particularly effusive taxicab driver, who drove us to dinner at Boat Quay, a picturesque waterfront location, spontaneously expressed his resentment towards what he referred to as the heavy-handed, overbearing attitude of the government. He made it clear, however, that he was not willing to rock the boat as long as the economy remained strong and his standard of living continued to improve. This seems to be the current view of most citizens; but, if economic conditions deteriorate, this cooperative spirit may be tested.

It's a Tough World Out There

Early in the new millennium Singapore was hurt by a weak worldwide economy and increasing regional and global terrorist activity. Many tourists curtailed their travel to Singapore and the country faced its most severe recession in four decades. To counteract these trends, which threatened the sense of economic well-being, Singapore began to broaden its economic development plans to incorporate another avenue for growth. Their first development plan was drawn up soon after gaining independence from Malaysia in 1965 and centered on creating a manufacturing base. The second phase, which began in the 1980s, concentrated on building a service sector. Recognizing the need for additional growth engines and the importance entrepreneurs play in an ultra-competitive global environment, Singapore has decided to promote innovation and enterprise development in their latest strategic plan. To this end, it has begun to encourage and nurture entrepreneurial start-ups and develop emerging industries.[36]

An eye-catching booklet published by Singapore's Economic Development Board states, "The entrepreneurial spirit is encouraged through national awards and cultivating an enterprising mind set in our young. Government rules and regulations are constantly reviewed to ensure that Singapore remains an ideal location to start, grow and globalize a business."[37] But here's the rub—the most creative and innovative entrepreneurs often have ideas and opinions that are out of the mainstream. They are usually attracted to regions that place a high value on personal freedom—something Singapore needs to foster. And entrepreneurs don't want a lot of restrictions on what they can say or do. Even with the best intentions, it is likely to be a major hurdle for staid Singapore to change its policies and culture so dramatically. As Tommy Koh has so clearly stated, "If Singapore is going to survive the new world, then we cannot have Singaporeans who are merely good at rote-learning. They must also be rounded and creative. Unless the government does so, we will never succeed in producing the kind of individuals that we need to power our economy in the next century."[38]

Lee Hsien Loong, the son of Singapore's founding father, Lee Kuan Yew, became prime minister in August of 2004. In a speech to graduates of Harvard University he spoke of pending government reforms—economic and social. Results to date are mixed; chewing gum, for example, can now be imported but only if it is sugar-free and sold exclusively in pharmacies. Of greater import, the government has signaled a more liberal attitude toward homosexuality after researchers discovered that cities with high concentrations of gay residents tended to exhibit higher levels of innovation. The jury is still out, but Singapore prides itself on being adaptable and, based upon what I observed, it would be unwise to bet against them.[39]

Two Countries, Two Cultures

For a good part of their recent history, Argentina has evidenced a deep-seated victim mentality. There is a widespread belief that their problems are caused by *THEM*—ineffective government officials (whom the citizens elected), corrupt business and labor leaders (who are tacitly condoned rather than prosecuted) and the IMF (whose money Argentina voluntarily requested to cover its profligate ways).

Singapore is a more difficult country to categorize. At first blush, it has the aura of an *US*-society with its widely proclaimed interest in the common good. Unfortunately, what serves the common good is determined, almost exclusively, by government officials. There is no guarantee that those in charge know what is best for the majority and, even if they did, other leaders, who may not be as wise, will eventually replace them. In addition, citizens are greatly constrained in expressing views that differ from the standard and harsh penalties can be imposed when some clearly debatable rules are transgressed. In other words, Singapore is effectively controlled by a relatively few people who demand that things be done exactly as they determine. People that demand one hundred percent allegiance to their point of view are usually *ME*-dominant. Even though the decisions of leaders may be made with the intent of serving the common good, their behavior has the effect of suppressing free choice. Free choice does have its messy baggage, but unless people are allowed to make their own decisions and mistakes they never learn, grow or achieve a sense of self-worth and self-fulfillment.

The introduction to the excellent book, *State-Society Relations in Singapore*, declares, "In a globalizing world, where access to worldwide information is now practically instantaneous, the need to develop citizens that can judge and make choices for themselves is increasingly recognized".[40] In other words, with vastly improved accessibility and sophistication of global communications a broad-based rather than hierarchical structure is essential. Where people lack empowerment, they gravitate toward satisfying their lower needs and gear their behavior to avoiding pain or gaining rewards. An imposed *US*-mentality isn't sustainable. Members of a society must be allowed to make choices, some of which will be self-ish, cause conflicts and be contrary to the greater good. Eventually the painful consequences that naturally follow from self-serving choices will encourage the development of a more inclusive, compassionate approach to life.

Argentina and Singapore's widely divergent personalities are obvious even to the most casual observer. And since integrating the best global values is at least as important as incorporating the best global business practices, perhaps both countries might profit from some global cross-fertilization. Singapore could sip a bit of Argentina's freewheeling, creative juices and Argentina could inhale a whiff of Singapore's highly disciplined, pragmatic atmosphere.

Notes

1. Tim Johnson, "Argentines Sinking Deeper," *The Philadelphia Inquirer*, 9 May 2002.
2. Luis Alberto Romero, *A History of Argentina in the Twentieth Century*, trans. James B. Brennan (University Park, PA: The Pennsylvania State University Press, 2002), 287–290.
3. Ibid., 296.
4. Johnson, "Argentines Sinking Deeper".
5. Romero, *A History of Argentina in the Twentieth Century*, 298.
6. Ibid., 313–314.
7. Ibid., 311.
8. Ibid., 337.
9. Ibid., 327.
10. Ibid., 344.
11. Stephen Spruiell, "The IMF and World Bank: an Overview," *A World Connected, http://www.aworldconnected.org/article.php?id=529*:16 December 2003.
12. "Argentina and the IMF: Which Is the Victim?" *The Economist*, 6 March 2004, 63.
13. Romero, *A History of Argentina in the Twentieth Century*, 344.
14. Ibid., 348.
15. Anthony Faiola, "Despair in Once-Proud Argentina: After Economic Collapse, Deep Poverty Makes Dignity a Casualty," *The Washington Post*, 6 August 2002, A1.
16. "Uruguay and Argentina: Don't Watch My Lips," *The Economist*, 8 June 2002, 34.
17. Marina Walker, "A Rising Star's Furious Fall to Hard Times," *The Philadelphia Inquirer*, 4 August 2002.

[18] Ana Campoy, "Latin Entrepreneurs Settle in U.S. Using Visa for Visiting Executives," *The Wall Street Journal*, 5 August 2002, A4.

[19] "The World Competitiveness Scoreboard 2004," *IMD-World Competitiveness Yearbook*, *http://www.imd.ch/documentswcy/content/ranking.pdf*: 4 May 2004.

[20] "Argentina Country Commercial Guide 2002," *http://www.usatrade.gov/website/cng.nsf/CCGurl/CCG-ARGENTINA2002-CH-2-00*:29 July 2002.

[21] "Uruguay and Argentina," 34.

[22] Johnson, "Argentines Sinking Deeper".

[23] "A Survey of Argentina: Crimes Past, Crimes Present," *The Economist*, 5 June 2004, 6.

[24] Santiago Fitapaldi, "Economic Recovery Leads to Argentine Amnesia," *Global Finance*, April 2004, 7.

[25] "A Survey of Argentina: the Insouciant Debtor," *The Economist*, 5 June 2004, 10.

[26] "2004 Index of Economic Freedom," *2004 Index of Economic Freedom—Search*, *http://cf.heritage.org/index/2004indexoffreedom.cfm*: The Heritage Foundation and the Wall Street Journal, 9 January 2004.

[27] "The World Competitiveness Scoreboard 2004."

[28] *Singapore's Enterprise Ecosystem—Yearbook 2001/02* (Singapore: Singapore Economic Development Board, September 2002), 15.

[29] Tommy Koh, interview by author, tape recording (Singapore: 22 November 2002).

[30] Buck Song Koh, interview by author, tape recording (Singapore: 19 November 2002).

[31] "Corruption Perceptions Index 2003," *Transparency International*, *http://www.tranparency.org/cpi/2003/cpi2003.en.html*: 7 October 2003.

[32] "How Bribery and Other Types of Corruption Threaten the Global Marketplace," *Inc: the Magazine for Growing Companies*, *http://www.inc.com/articles/global/24749.html*: 3 December 2002, 5.

[33] Ibid.

[34] "Singapore Won't Relax Laws on Public Speaking," *The International Herald Tribune* (Paris), 27 November 2002.

[35] Associated Press, "Bloomberg Apologizes to Singapore," *Yahoo! News*, *http://story.news.yahoo.com/news*: 26 August 2002.

[36] Singapore's Enterprise Ecosystem—Yearbook, 12.

[37] Ibid., 49.

[38] Tommy Koh, "Reflections on Civil Society," in *State-Society Relations in Singapore*, ed. Gillian Koh and Ooi Goik Ling (Singapore: Oxford University Press, 2000), 233.

[39] "The Son Rises," *The Economist*, 24 July 2004, 39.

[40] Gillian Koh and Ooi Giok Ling, "Achieving State-Society Synergies," in *State-Society Relations in Singapore*, ed. Gillian Koh and Ooi Goik Ling (Singapore: Oxford University Press, 2000), 10.

Chapter Seven

NationDividers

Recently, my wife, son and I spent two captivating weeks in South Africa. We traveled throughout the country from Kruger National Park in the east to Cape Town in the southwest speaking to a variety of individuals. We heard the life experiences of everyone from apartheid-era prisoners to influential business executives. Most people appear to be working hard to stitch together the fragments of their turbulent past. A short history of South Africa's development will help put today's events in context and clarify the significant challenges this extraordinarily beautiful, recently rejuvenated country now encounters. We will then discuss the legacies of apartheid and the valuable lessons they provide for the global community.

Planting Seeds of Destruction

The seeds of the tensions between the native blacks and the European settlers were originally planted early in the colonial era. These tensions grew until, in 1946, police precipitated a bloodbath by opening fire on 70,000 striking black miners. This hastened the preoccupation of the white electorate with racial issues that have dominated South Africa's history, culture and economy until recently. The National Party (NP) swept into power and instituted its policy of apartheid, a word that literally means separateness. The underlying assumption of Apartheid was that European (white) culture represented the peak of human development and that the isolation of inferior (black) cultures should be encouraged. By 1951 a series of bills enforcing apartheid had been enacted. The Immorality and Mixed Marriages Act forbade people of different races from marrying or sleeping together; the Population Registration Act required that all South Africans be classified into one of four government-defined racial groups; the Group Areas Act partitioned people into designated areas based on their racial makeup; and the Unlawful Organizations and Suppression of Communism Acts prohibited Communist party activities. In 1956, Coloureds (mixed-race) were disenfranchised and a process was begun to forcibly remove people from parts of white inhabited cities. As the NP aggressively pursued its ultra-racial policies, the African National Congress (ANC), influenced by Gandhi's passive resistance, was rapidly gaining popularity. In March 1960, a peaceful protest ended in violence and the death of 69 blacks. The government declared a state of emergency and within weeks the two largest black political parties (the ANC and its offshoot, the Pan African Congress) were banned. The ANC sensed that peaceful protests weren't working quickly enough and began terrorist attacks against government installations such as post offices and police stations. Organization leaders were eventually captured and taken into custody; the most prominent, Nelson Mandela, was sentenced to life imprisonment.[1]

Robben Island is a small windswept parcel of land about seven miles off the coast of South Africa near Cape Town. It became the place where South Africa's apartheid regime sequestered its political prisoners; Mandela was sent to the island in 1962 and remained there until the early 1980s. We toured the island with a guide who, as a former prisoner, was able to describe his life as an inmate in graphic terms. He matter-of-factly related the dreadful conditions the prisoners faced: loss of personal control, isolation and arbitrary punishment, capricious and discriminatory rules and insensitive, vindictive guards and warden. The facilities were cold and sparse; even worse than I had imagined. As we filed out of the prison our tour guide concluded his presentation with the poignant words, "We have forgiven but will never forget."

Back to the Past

International outcries denouncing South Africa's apartheid policies began in the 1960s with a variety of boycotts. In 1971, Burton Malkiel, then Chairman of the Economics Department at Princeton University, gave a talk to the Endowment Conference in New York City. He described how a group of students at Princeton demanded that the University sell its stock holdings in firms with subsidiaries or affiliates operating in South Africa. The students argued that these companies were effectively supporting the racist government and profiting immorally from such investments. The controversy caused quite a stir. While the committee charged with making recommendations to the University voted against selling any shares, it did recommend, in unequivocal terms, that the University denounce irresponsible corporate practices.[2] Their report said in part, "Particularly, we abhor the practices of several U.S. banks in granting South Africa a substantial line of credit, which helped bolster the shaky government after the Sharpsville massacre of 1960."[3] This report turned out to have considerable relevance. In June 2002, some 30 years after the Princeton committee raised the issue, a class action lawsuit, seeking billions of dollars in reparations, was filed by four black South Africans against Citigroup and Swiss banking giants UBS and Credit Suisse. The suit alleges that the three companies, among others, helped prop up a struggling and discriminatory white government. It points out that their loans came after the United Nations had asked all member states to break off relations. According to the lawsuit, "Were it not for the conspiracy of these financial institutions and companies, apartheid would not have been kept alive."[4] While the merits and ultimate disposition of this lawsuit are uncertain, the potential ramifications should give pause to every global company.

In response to the committee recommendation, Princeton's President, Robert F. Goheen, sent a letter to corporations whose stock was held in the university's investment portfolio urging the companies to improve the way they treated black workers. While responses from the corporate community varied, at least some of the companies initiated programs to improve the wages and working conditions of non-whites in South Africa.[5] Sometime after Princeton's announcement one of my clients requested that any company doing business in South Africa be eliminated from her portfolio. This was my first introduction to the concept of socially responsible investing (SRI) and it has had a significant impact on the types of investments I have made over the last 30 years. SRI, when used in conjunction with product boycotts of socially irresponsible companies, has had an increasingly significant impact on all types of corporate policies.

Injustice at its Worst

June 16, 1976—the Soweto Uprising—stands as a defining moment in South Africa's troubled history. The best way to learn about this historic event was to take a personal tour of Soweto. Our guide, who lives in the area, told us some of the history; in the 1800s, with the coming of the European settlers, thousands of blacks were stripped of their land and forced to find work in the minefields near Johannesburg. As more and more settled in inner-city slums, concerns of the segregationist government about the proximity of blacks to white suburbs grew until, in 1930, an answer was found. A farm, 11 miles to the southwest of Johannesburg, was designated as a new township (with no roads, no electricity, no running water) and blacks living in and around the city were served with eviction papers. Not surprisingly, most people refused to move. So, in 1933, the government enacted the Slums Clearance Act and forcibly evicted blacks from the inner cities. Defeated, the new homeless moved to the township, and Soweto, acronym for Southwestern Township, was born.[6]

At the Hector Pieterson Memorial—erected in 1996 to commemorate the uprising—I learned that, in 1974, the white minority government declared that Afrikaans would become the language of instruction for blacks. Students objected to being taught in the language of their oppressor. Many teachers could not speak Afrikaans, but were now required to use it to teach all subjects. In addition, this stipulation meant that courses in all black schools would be taught in Afrikaans even though college courses at the universities that blacks were allowed to attend would be taught in English. As a consequence blacks, lacking the necessary language skills, would not be able to get into any university. Thousands of students in Soweto boycotted classes to show their anger against this repugnant policy.

On June 16, 1976, police opened fire on hundreds of Soweto school children that were peacefully protesting the Afrikaans decree. Children turned on their parents, something hitherto unheard of in traditional society, and destroyed everything they could that belonged to the municipal authority—schools, post offices and the ubiquitous shebeens (beer halls). The police retaliated with brutal assaults, arrests and killings. The memorial square and the neighboring museum (opened on Heritage Day—September 24, 2001—the 25th anniversary of the uprising) feature moving photographs taken by famous black photographers, including the infamous shot of Hector Pieterson—one of the young boys who died in a hail of police bullets—being carried by a young man whose face is contorted in disbelief and pain. Hector's sister runs alongside, her mouth a silent wail of grief.[7] These photographs offer a window on the anger, the fear, the aggression and the grief of these times, after which Soweto and South Africa were never to be the same. It wasn't until six months later that the uprising subsided and the casualties could be counted. Seven hundred people were dead, thousands of children detained, 500 teachers resigned and irate protesters gutted hundreds of vehicles and buildings.[8] The damage from the Soweto protests, both physical and psychological, was devastating. What started as a student rebellion against apartheid had consequences far more profound than those early rebels ever imagined. Black education facilities had been totally ruined and a generation of black teenagers had their schooling irreparably disrupted. Some of the consequences and tragic aftermath of this episode would be far reaching.

Defying Expectations

The conservative-leaning F. W. de Klerk became President in 1989 and, contrary to most expectations, lifted the ban on the ANC, the PAC and 20 other organizations on February 2, 1990. The National Party soon announced that it was ready to negotiate a new constitution with the ANC and other interested parties. Within a relatively short period of time, Nelson Mandela was released from 27 years of imprisonment, the national state of emergency was rescinded, apartheid laws were repealed one by one and the ANC abandoned its armed struggle. The first Convention for a Democratic South Africa

(CoDeSA) began in December 1991. Late in 1992, the ANC and the NP agreed to a five-year government of national unity and a resumption of multi-party CoDeSA negotiations. April 27, 1994, the first South African all-party Election Day, turned out to be quite peaceful. The ANC won with 62 percent of the vote and quickly installed Nelson Mandela as the first black president of South Africa.[9]

The international community normalized diplomatic and economic relations with South Africa immediately following the 1994 elections. The new government faced a number of complicated economic and social problems. In spite of the lip service paid to free market concepts by the apartheid-era government, the economy was primarily state controlled. In addition, many ANC leaders had been in exile for years in the Soviet Union and its satellite states and returned to South Africa with a predilection for centralized economic planning and the nationalization of industry. Before long, however, the ANC began to see the merits of a market-driven economy and supported, at least partially, the privatization of a variety of firms.[10] Thabo Mbeki, the former Deputy President who succeeded Mandela in 1999, shifted the attention of government from political reconciliation to economic transformation. The government recognized that fostering economic growth and development is the most effective way to create badly needed jobs and begin to narrow the wide disparity between rich and poor.

Separate But Grossly Unequal

Decades of racially biased government policies left an indelible mark on every facet of South African life. Dysfunctional families and malnourished children were symptoms of the yawning gap between the few enormously wealthy and the vast majority who live in abject poverty. The gap in education levels is nearly as wide. The strife that exists between labor and management reflects the exploitation and resulting distrust that developed during the years of white domination. And while the HIV/AIDS epidemic can't be tied to apartheid policies, many commentators blame the early reluctance of the government to acknowledge and attack the problem to a fear among blacks that this was another attempt by the white minority to put blacks down and make them feel inferior. The wealth, health and education gaps have severely curtailed South Africa's ability to integrate into the world economy. These gaps can only be closed if South Africa's citizens are able to achieve the economic benefits they have been long denied.

Educational Impoverishment

The educational legacy of apartheid is also a major obstacle to South Africa's rejuvenation and its ability to compete on a global scale. Until 1953, there was effectively no government-sponsored education for black Africans. A black education department was then established; part of the enabling legislation stated, "Natives (blacks) must be taught from early age that equality with Europeans (whites) is not for them."[11] The education provided as a result of this supposedly forward-looking policy was, therefore, substandard for a generation before Afrikaans was declared the language of instruction. The student boycotts, which began in Soweto in the mid-1970s, spread to many other black enclaves, adding to the already sizable number of undereducated citizens. It has been estimated that over 10 percent of the population is completely illiterate. Today, spending on education in South Africa is above international norms and universal education is an important goal; nevertheless, poverty, inconvenient school locations, children who are orphaned or suffer from physical disabilities all work against the achievement of the government's targets.[12]

The schools today, while still primitive by developed country standards, are definitely improving. The student-teacher ratio varies from a very respectable 15:1 to a not so encouraging 40:1. Unfortunately many teachers have inadequate training and some work for little if any salary as the education authorities lack adequate funding. Many schools are without electricity, water and even toilets. A school I visited, Hananani Primary School, is located in a small rural village near the boundary of the Sabi Sand Wildlife Reserve. Thanks to some generous community donations, electricity was recently installed (a first step for a project sponsored by the Gates Foundation to provide computers). But running water is still not available and one room, not much bigger than a living room in an upscale U.S. home, accommodates all grades with a curtain that can be drawn to separate the grade levels.

True to the intention of the apartheid government, many blacks still lack basic skills save that of laborer. Coincident with an exceedingly high black unemployment rate, there is a dearth of people qualified to fill vacancies in high-tech industries, engineering, finance and medicine. High unemployment leads to high levels of poverty; South Africa has one of the widest disparities between rich and poor of any country in the world. Driving down the major highway that leads to Cape Town, I viewed the township of Khayelitsha, miles and miles of pint-sized, tin-roofed shacks crammed on top of one another like sardines in a can. Filth and squalor envelop these squatter camps from one end to the other; it looks like a slight breeze would bring the shanties down like a house of cards. To see so many people living in such utter poverty is heart wrenching and this distressing image stayed in my mind for a long time. Poverty breeds despair and often leads to lawlessness; hence the notoriously high levels of crime, particularly in the major urban centers of South Africa. Compounding the problem, according to the U.S. Department of State, is the fact that, in many communities, the police are neither accepted nor effective because of their historic role in enforcing minority rule.[13] Given a dearth of skilled labor and a crime rate that engenders palpable fear in natives and visitors alike, foreign investment has been severely undermined. Investment capital is well known for being cowardly; it goes where it feels the most secure. With the global demand for investment capital far exceeding the supply, investors have the luxury of being very selective. South Africa needs to attract capital to grow and thrive; the only way to do this is to break the apartheid-induced spiral of substandard education, deplorable poverty and intolerable levels of crime.

To its credit, the government has made improving the lives of the millions of poor South Africans the centerpiece of its multifaceted and challenging agenda. Obviously, progress in solving the significant social problems requires increased government revenue. But again the legacy of apartheid hinders this effort. White deception, black defiance and government indifference (part of the apartheid legacy) make the job of collecting taxes from those legally required to pay harder than necessary. As an example, about 6 million people, or half the working population, have not registered to pay taxes. While the amount of legally required tax revenue that is lost each year due to underreporting is not precisely known, most agree it is substantial. New technology and stricter enforcement are gradually narrowing this tax gap. What is also needed is a change in attitude where citizens see paying their fair share of taxes as a legal obligation and a civic responsibility.[14]

Working Apart

Another by-product of apartheid is the unusually contentious relationship between management and labor. Throughout the period of white minority rule, apartheid laws encouraged the exploitation of black workers. Working conditions were deplorable and wages, both absolute and relative to white workers, were low. As a result, labor developed a marked distrust of the motivations and intentions of

most employers. Labor unions are now operating in a surplus labor environment, as the South African unemployment rate is exceedingly high. Therefore, trade unions,
which have long been major supporters of the powerful
African National Congress, have used their considerable
political clout to push for restrictive labor laws and regulations. These laws have made unskilled labor costly to
employ and difficult to terminate.[15]

An additional dimension of the problem was brought to
my attention when I spoke with a financial executive working for a multi-national gold mining company with investments in South Africa. She pointed out that black workers
are still discriminated against by the imposition of strictly
structured job titles based on skill level and education. Even
a college degree has significant value only if it was obtained
from a select group of universities (most of which have few
black students). And blacks are not the only group disadvantaged in post-apartheid industry; years of discrimination
by white males has made it very difficult for females to break
into the management ranks or be taken seriously once they
are there. My contact related an experience she had while
attending a meeting. A male manager first questioned her
position of authority and then grilled her about her qualifications. When she later presented her impressive resume, he
said he only wanted to know whether she was important
enough for him to refrain from offending her.

The crux of the conflict between labor and management
revolves around the different priorities assigned to somewhat similar objectives. Both parties are interested in job creation, a more equitable distribution of wealth and economic
growth. The trade unions make job creation their top priority and often oppose policies that will, even temporarily,
reduce or eliminate jobs. Unions are generally opposed to
privatizing state-owned assets even if this will eventually
make jobs more secure and/or create more employment

opportunities. Business groups, on the other hand, place economic growth at the head of their list as they see a growing economy as a prerequisite for sustainable job growth. They recognized that, with South Africa's untenable wealth gap, efficiency has to take a back seat to greater social equity. In these cases, transparent government subsidies are preferable to propping up bloated, uncompetitive companies. The former approach reveals the true price of income redistribution and enables the costs and benefits to be objectively evaluated.

South Africa's trade unions might find it instructive to study the history of the labor movement in the United States. Unions were an essential counterweight to exploitive corporate practices in the early years of the labor movement in the United States. Over time, however, unions used their increasing power and influence to secure prohibitively expensive labor contracts—the costs of which were far in excess of productivity gains. In the steel industry, for instance, wages reached levels that made domestic steel uncompetitive with foreign producers. With imports more economical, union jobs declined precipitously. The rise and fall of the United States steel industry is a classic example of how shortsighted, *ME*-oriented union practices not only destroyed many jobs but diminished union influence.

Because the influence of labor in South African politics is so formidable, unions have been instrumental in influencing legislation that pushes labor costs to counterproductive levels. In fact, the cost of labor relative to capital about doubled in the 1990s.[16] In order to compete globally, South African companies have found it more profitable to invest in machinery rather than additional workers. This has been a boon to productivity but has not helped the severe unemployment problem. Until trade union attitudes change and allow businesses more flexible work rules and more liberal restructuring and privatization opportunities, unemployment is likely to remain disturbingly high and foreign investment will be constrained. Whether businesses prosper or fail depends in large part on how well management and labor can understand each other's needs and find ways to work together for their mutual benefit.

Creating a Rainbow Coalition

The National Economic Development and Labor Council (Nedlac) was organized in 1995 to bring together groups with divergent objectives and priorities, two of the most important being management and labor. Nedlac is an outgrowth of the struggle against apartheid and unilateral government decision-making. The impetus for creating Nedlac was the desire by all segments of South Africa's society to make decisions in a more inclusive, transparent manner. There was also the recognition that successful economic, social and development policies can best be achieved through a process of consensus building. In addition to representation from government, business and labor, Nedlac includes organizations that represent a variety of South African community interests. Through negotiations, consultations, information sharing, research and dispute resolution the four special interest groups consider proposed labor legislation and significant changes to social and economic policy before they are implemented or introduced in Parliament.[17] As Raymond Parsons, Overall Business Convenor stated in a Nedlac annual report, "Effective social dialogue can be a valuable way of taking a holistic view of what needs to be done. The quality of Nedlac's outcomes hinges to a large extent on the capacity of stakeholders to contribute constructively to the social dialogue process, to look beyond their immediate interests, and to find acceptable solutions where possible."[18]

In order to get a better understanding of Nedlac's successes and challenges, I met with Friede Dowie, Secretary-General of Business South Africa (BSA). BSA represents 19 employer federations and is one of two business organizations representing the business constituency in Nedlac. Dowie discussed two of the most contentious issues facing this loosely knit alliance—black empowerment and privatization of state-owned enterprises.[19]

Power to the People

Black empowerment is a term that describes the effort to increase the ownership of the black majority in the private sector and, thereby, broaden South Africa's economic base. The share of capital currently held by blacks is paltry and the black ownership of the stocks listed on the Johannesburg Stock Exchange is minuscule.[20] Many people, both inside and outside the government, are concerned that the ownership of big industries, where the majority of the wealth resides, is not being redistributed fast enough. Thus the government began negotiating with South Africa's major industries to establish targets for transferring a specific level of ownership, i.e. 25 percent, to non-whites within a fixed time frame, often 10 years.[21] There appears to be no intention to expropriate capital; the government wants owners to be compensated for any transfer of wealth. And there is the realization, at least in some quarters, that faster economic growth would be a big aid in smoothing the transition. The biggest obstacle to accomplishing the black empowerment goal is finding a way to finance this transfer of capital. A great deal of money is required and the banks are understandably reluctant to be the sole facilitators. Nonetheless, through a variety of innovative approaches, progress is being made. As long as the ownership transfer is predictable and doesn't, at least initially, require a complete change of control, most industry executives seem to accept the process as necessary, if not desirable.

Working Together

Joint ventures, encouraged by government procurement rules that favor black-controlled companies, are one promising approach to black empowerment. In 2002, for example, when the government offered to sell the rights to set up a second telecommunications company to qualified bidders, it stipulated that a black-owned partner would have to own 19 percent of the company.[22] Privatization is another important tool. But, according to Dowie, unions would not even discuss the concept in the early days of Nedlac. Restructuring was the only allowed terminology and inherent in its use was the assumption that control of a restructured firm would always remain in the public sector.[23] The Congress of South African Trade Unions (Cosatu) is now willing to discuss privatizations provided the privatized assets do not include essential services or the state enterprise being privatized clearly lacks commercial viability. Cosatu does not yet seem ready to accept the concept that the private sector is generally more efficient in serving the needs of the citizens, particularly the disadvantaged.[24]

Telkom, South Africa's leading integrated communications operator is an excellent example of a government-owned company that moved toward privatization by bringing in foreign investors. In the early 1990s Telkom and the Post Office were separated from the colossus that ran apartheid era communications. Approximately five years later, the government sold a 30 percent interest in Telkom to Thintana Communications LLC, a consortium of SBC Communications Inc. and Telkom Malaysia Berhad, for 6 billion rand. The new international partners signed a strategic services agreement that brought some 75 employees and a great deal of telecommunications know-how to South Africa.[25] Over the next several years the equity investors helped Telkom modernize its network by upgrading its technology, raising overall skill levels, providing knowledge

of industry best practices and introducing sophisticated marketing expertise. At a meeting I had with several of Telkom's
U.S. executives, I was impressed by their dedication to
improving South Africa's telephone service as well as the
pride they took in being able to make a meaningful contribution to South Africa's economic development. According
to Sizwe Nxasana, CEO of Telkom, five years ago he was
inundated with complaints about the company. "You meet
with the same customers today and they rave," Nxasana says
with understandable pride.[26] While the rising price of phone
service—needed to offset the costs associated with double-
digit inflation and system wide modernization—has upset
some customers, the benefits of the global transfer of technology and capital are clearly evident.

In the first quarter of 2003, the government used the initial public offering of Telkom stock as a tool to improve its
Black Empowerment program. Officials embarked on a campaign to build awareness of the benefits of long-term stock
investment and strong capital markets and to encourage a
culture of saving. While all South African citizens were eli-
gible to buy shares at prices below those offered to international financial institutions, lower-income and historically
disadvantaged individuals (those unable to vote before 1994)
received a greater discount and were offered loyalty incentives for keeping their investments for a specified period of
time. The government instituted a large-scale media campaign aimed not only at adults but students as well. Teachers
were trained to use specially developed booklets on financial
literacy and a series of community-based activities was
designed to make non-traditional investors aware of this
wide-ranging educational initiative. A statement issued by
the Public Enterprises Minister summarized the multifaceted objectives of the government: "As we refocus the role of
the state to take the plight of the poor seriously, we also
unlock increasing opportunities for expanding ownership of

wealth through black economic empowerment and for improving the efficiency and performance of state-owned enterprises."[27]

It's a War

HIV/AIDS is a worldwide crisis; it can't, therefore, be linked to apartheid *per se*. But many would argue that this health catastrophe has become more dire in South Africa because of a post-apartheid phobia. Specifically, Thabo Mbeki, South Africa's President, initially downplayed the seriousness of the illness, in part, because apartheid-era scientists purportedly tried to produce and disseminate viruses that would kill only black Africans. In addition, early in the 1990s the then-ruling National Party alleged that ANC leaders (such as Mbeki), who had been exiled in other parts of Africa, were carrying AIDS into the country. Mbeki is, therefore, sensitive to any insinuation that Africans are diseased and has not been as aggressive in publicizing and attacking the disease as many would have liked.[28] Despite initial reluctance on the part of the government to tackle the problem aggressively, progress in increasing AIDS awareness is being made. Educational billboards pointing out the risks of HIV and the need for preventive measures are widespread. Traffic lights in Soweto even have the word AIDS inscribed in the upper red light so that drivers are constantly reminded about the need to STOP AIDS. In response to pressure from many quarters, the government has committed to reinvigorate its HIV/AIDS program with substantial increases in funding in future years.

A few statistics will graphically illustrate the scope of the disease and should convince even the most skeptical that the situation requires immediate attention. The disease has already killed hundreds of thousands of South Africans and, based on a variety of estimates, could claim another 4 to 5 million lives (11 percent of the population) by 2010. There are currently some 300,000 households headed by orphaned children and, before long, there could be close to a million orphans under 15 years of age. Ill health exacerbates the already severe poverty problem and is hitting hard at the teaching and nursing professions as well as the army and police forces. HIV/AIDS is likely to have a profound effect on business and thereby South Africa's effort to create jobs and improve social equity. The number of employees lost to AIDS over the next decade could reach 40 to 50 percent of the work force at some companies, and, during the same period, approximately 15 percent of the South Africa's highly-skilled employees are projected to contract HIV.[29]

Spurred on by regulatory bodies and their own self-interest, South African businesses are accelerating their response to the AIDS crisis. The Johannesburg Stock Exchange has insisted that companies report on how AIDS affects their overall business, their markets and their workers and spell out how they are working to combat the disease. A majority of South Africa's largest firms have adopted formal HIV/AIDS policies, realizing that, as the number of people with AIDS increases, they will be faced with diminished productivity, declining morale, rising absenteeism, the loss of valuable skills and soaring retraining costs. Moreover, the fears of foreign investors can be more easily allayed when the extent of the problem is fully disclosed. Business is taking a proactive role, but they cannot do it alone; only a partnership with government and labor can result in a comprehensive and effective HIV/AIDS policy.[30] Despite a multitude of problems, South Africa is making steady, if measured, social and economic progress.

South Africa celebrated a decade of democracy in 2004. The country has a free press, active social pressure groups, independent courts and, in April 2004, successfully conducted its third all-race election. Democracy, however, loses a good part of its luster when a substantial number of citizens are mired in abject poverty. Shortly after his 2004 re-election, President Thabo Mbeki detailed a series of steps aimed at halving the countries massive unemployment by boosting economic growth. Given the divisive legacy of apartheid, the task will be hard and success gradual.

An Obvious Conclusion

Many people believe that the keys to happiness are succinctly captured by the phrase, "Health, Wealth and the Wisdom to enjoy them." If so, South Africa, despite its incredible beauty, abundant natural resources and goodhearted people, still has considerable hurdles to overcome. Health in the country is fragile, its wealth is untenably concentrated and its population so poorly educated that many have trouble discerning wisdom from folly. While apartheid can't be blamed for every problem, it is connected in some fashion to most challenges facing the country. Every step South Africa makes toward participation in an expanding global economy is hindered by the legacies of apartheid. South Africa clearly illustrates that wherever separation—ethnic, racial, religious or any other of its insidious forms—is enforced or condoned, the consequences are severe and unrelenting. Thinking only about *ME*; that is, my safety, security and material well-being, to the detriment of the rest of *US*, is patently foolish and, inevitably self-defeating. The lesson of South Africa's reprehensible past is powerful—but so is the courageous struggle of her people to repudiate it and become productive partners in the global economy.

Notes

[1] Philip Briggs, *Guide to South Africa*, 2nd ed. (Bucks, England: Bradt Publications, 1994), 12–14.

[2] Burton G. Malkiel, "Socially Responsible Investing," in *Classics II: Another Investor's Anthology*, ed. Charles D. Ellis with James R. Vertin (Homewood IL: Business One Irwin, 1991), 605.

[3] Malkiel, "Socially Responsible Investing," 609.
[4] Ravi Nessman, Associated Press, "Financial Firms to be Sued Over Apartheid," *The Philadelphia Inquirer*, 18 June 2002, A14.
[5] Ibid., 609.
[6] Pippa de Bruyn, *Frommer's South Africa*, 2nd ed. (New York: Hungry Minds, Inc., 2001), 79.
[7] Ibid., 80.
[8] Briggs, Guide to South Africa, 14.
[9] Ibid., 16–20.
[10] "Country Commercial Guide South Africa 2002," *Chapter 3: Political Environment, http://www.usatrade.gov/website/cng.nsf/ccgurl/ccg-south_ africa2002-ch-3:29:* July 2002, 1–2.
[11] "June 16th Student Uprising—Part I: Background to the Uprising," *African History, http://africanhistory.about.com/library/weekly/aa06001a.htm*: 9 December 2002, 1.
[12] Kader Asmal, "Private Sector Help Needed for Schooling," *Financial Mail*, 8 November 2002, 20.
[13] Gerald P. O'Driscoll Jr., Kim R. Holmes and Mary A. O'Grady, *2002 Index of Economic Freedom* (The Heritage Foundation and the Wall Street Journal, 2002), 362.
[14] Henri E. Cauvin, "Taxes are Helping Right Some of Apartheid's Old Wrongs," *The New York Times*, 15 September 2002.
[15] "Jobless and Joyless," *The Economist*, 22 February 2001.
[16] Ibid.
[17] *Nedlac Annual Report 2002* (Saxonwold, South Africa, 2002), 7.
[18] Ibid., 5.
[19] Friede Dowie, interview by author, tape recording (Rosebank, South Africa:13 November 2002).
[20] "Shades of Grey," *The Economist*, 7 September 2002, 59.
[21] Ibid.
[22] Ibid.
[23] Dowie.
[24] Karl Gostner, "Privatisation the Bottom Line," *Enterprise* (Houghton, South Africa), November 2002, 20–26.
[25] "Company Profile," *Telkom, http://www.telkom.co.za.company/ profile.jsp*: 14 December 2002.
[26] David Shapshak, "Green Fingers," *African Communications* (Cape Town, South Africa), Issue 3/2002, 18.
[27] Jeff Radebe, "Media Statement," *Department of Public Enterprises, Republic of South Africa, http://www.telkomshareoffer.co.za*: 4 June 2003.
[28] "In Mandela's Shadow," *The Economist,* 14 December 2002, 23.
[29] "South African HIV/ AIDS Statistics," material compiled by Fleishman Hillard, South Africa (November 2002).
[30] "Strategic Caring," *The Economist*, 5 October 2002, 64.

PART THREE

THE FLAWS AND CONSEQUENCES

"If we continue to believe as we have always believed, we will continue to act as we have always acted. If we continue to act as we have always acted, we will continue to get what we have always gotten."

JOHN D. ADAMS, PH.D., AUTHOR
THINKING TODAY AS IF
TOMORROW MATTERED

Chapter Eight

TerrorIsms

A n "ism" is an extreme position usually focused on a single criterion rather than an overall structure. As such it is contrary to a unified view of life; it neglects factors critical to equity and sustainability. This chapter looks at egotism, idealism, protectionism, escapism and separatism and how they relate to previous chapters on EntrepreneurCelebs, EcoIdealists, PoliticalShortimers, BlameGamers and NationDividers. The concept of terrorism, which is, in many respects, a derivative of the first five isms is also explored.[1]

Egotism

Self-interest, narrowly defined, is the guiding principle of egotism. The egotist is driven by a desire for self-preservation and by an exclusive reliance on sense-based reasoning. Thus, such a person will, at various times, believe that his or her self-interest is dependent on physical well-being, power, pleasure, fame or fortune.[2]

An egotist tends to be conceited and selfish and often develops an exaggerated sense of self-importance. The early years of the 21st century are replete with examples of headline-grabbing corporate officers whose self-serving actions reached egregious levels. With the bull market of the late 1990s and the growing popularity of business publications and TV shows, many top executives attained star status. Unfortunately they began to believe their inflated press clippings and coveted celebrity over entrepreneurship. As company stocks soared, some top executives believed there was no limit to their worth. In addition to extravagant multimillion-dollar compensation packages, many captains of industry extracted perks that even royalty would find embarrassing. Seven- and eight-figure corporate loans routinely forgiven; lavishly furnished second homes complete with food, wine, flowers and staff; free use of company jets, helicopters, limos and security personnel; memberships at exclusive clubs and complimentary seats to a variety of entertainment venues are a few of the opulent extras heaped on many high level executives. Greed and hubris infiltrated executive suites, followed by high-level resignations and corporate retrenchment or collapse. WorldCom, Enron, Vivendi and Adelphia are a few of the fallen idols either struggling to survive or burdened by bankruptcy.

Many executives became so uncompromisingly *ME*-oriented that achieving personal fame and fortune took precedence over the success of the company. "I need," "I want," "I am entitled" were the childish and inevitably self-destructive demands of these immature personalities. Abraham Zeleznik, a psychoanalyst and professor emeritus at Harvard Business School, explained the meaning of the word entitlement as follows: "By entitlements I mean an aspect of a narcissistic personality who comes to believe that he and the institutions are one" and therefore "that he can take what he wants when he wants it."[3] As a result, **ME** personalities get sloppy with the allocation of their time, imprudent with company money and indiscriminate with regard to right and wrong, ethical and unethical, legal and illegal.

Egotistical hubris is not the exclusive domain of business people. Anyone can be drawn in to this seductive black hole. The story below is a good illustration of how shameless **ME**-driven behavior led to unintended consequences.

A Charlotte, NC lawyer purchased a box of very rare and expensive cigars; he then insured them against fire, among other things. Within a month of having smoked his entire stockpile of these rare cigars and without having made even his first premium payment on the policy, the lawyer filed an insurance claim. In his claim, the lawyer stated the cigars were lost "in a series of small fires."

The insurance company refused to pay, citing the obvious reason: that the man had consumed the cigars in the normal fashion. The lawyer sued... and won! In delivering the ruling the judge agreed with the insurance company that the claim was frivolous. The judge stated nevertheless, that the lawyer held a policy from the company in which it had warranted that the cigars were insurable and also guaranteed that it would insure them against fire, without defining what it considered to be "unacceptable fire" and was obligated to pay the claim.

Rather than endure a lengthy and costly appeal process, the insurance company accepted the ruling and paid $15,000 to the lawyer for the rare cigars lost in the "fires." After the lawyer cashed the check, the insurance company had him arrested on 24 counts of ARSON!!! With his own insurance company claim plus testimony *from the previous case, the lawyer was convicted of intentionally burning his insured property and he was sentenced to 24 months in jail and ordered to pay a $24,000.00 fine.*

This story, though unverified, is purportedly the 1st place winner in a Criminal Lawyers Award Contest. The lawyer's arrogant behavior and his subsequent downfall are an excellent example of what happens when blatant egotism takes over. In contrast, according to Jim Collins' book, *Good to Great*, the people behind most successful businesses are humble, reserved, gracious, unpretentious and unimpressed by any of their press clippings.[4]

Idealism

Idealism is a consistent commitment to specific principles. Sometimes those principles are universal in nature and sometimes they are more parochial, subject to interpretation and personal judgments. Idealists are driven by deeply held values and specific rules of conduct and they are not deterred by past relationships or popular outcomes. Idealists can be rigid and inflexible and, at times, oblivious to the effect their decisions have on themselves or others.[5]

Environmental activists, for example, tend to be idealists concerned with the effect human actions have on the totality of things—the whole planet, the entire solar system, life in its myriad forms. They see an undeniable connection between everything that happens and, in this sense, feel they are motivated by a concern for all of **US**. There are, however, some problems with such highly principled positions. No human being sees the whole picture and, despite the best intentions, mistakes in judgment can be made. Our beliefs have all been conditioned to some extent by our family background, our personal experiences and our cultural heritage. Unless we allow new information or experiences into our lives, we cannot accept the possibility of different conclusions.

The following anonymous story illustrates how individuals from different cultures can have the same goal but entirely different plans for achieving their objectives.

An American businessman was at the pier of a Mexican coastal village when a small boat with just one fisherman docked. Inside the boat were several large yellowfin tuna. The American commented on the quality of the fish and asked how long it took to catch them.

The Mexican replied, "Only a little while."

The American then asked why didn't he stay out longer and catch more fish?

The Mexican said he had enough to support his family's immediate needs. The American then asked, "But what do you do with the rest of your time?"

The fisherman said, "I sleep late, fish a little, play with my children, take a siesta with my wife, Maria. I have a full and busy life, señor."

The American scoffed. "You should spend more time fishing and with the proceeds buy a bigger boat, with the proceeds from the bigger catch you could buy several boats, soon you would have a fleet of fishing boats. Instead of selling your catch to a middleman you would sell directly to the processor, eventually opening your own cannery. You would need to leave this small coastal fishing village and move to Mexico City, then LA and eventually NYC where you would run your expanding enterprise."

"But señor, how long will all this take?"

The American replied, "15–20 years."

"But what then, señor?"

The American laughed and said, "That's the best part. When the time is right you would sell your company's stock to the public and become very rich. You would make millions."

"Millions, señor? Then what?"

The American said, "Then you would retire. Move to a small coastal fishing village where you would sleep late, fish a little, play with your kids, take a siesta with your wife."[6]

Idealists often focus solely on some utopian vision and disregard practical considerations. Such behavior has value as it makes others aware of their prejudices and more conscious of the ramifications of their actions. Sometimes, a situation becomes so extreme that unequivocal declarations are required to capture the attention of the majority. Take the case of Greenpeace in the early years of its existence; the confrontational posture may have been necessary to focus attention on the appalling degradation of the environment and compel people to reassess the urgency of the situation. In today's world, however, malicious measures often cause a backlash that does more harm to the cause of the organization. As an example, a number of radical underground environmentalists have "spiked" trees (planted hidden metal bars in the trunks) to protest logging. This not only cripples chain saws but can also result in serious injury to workers. In the space of a few years, an estimated $45 million worth of damage was inflicted on North American properties by these fanatical idealists bent on inflicting severe damage on those they believe are the enemies of the environment.[7] For the most part, the *either/or* world of the radical idealist doesn't result in much more than harsh counter attacks and hardened positions. If idealists presented their cause in a still vigorous but more thoughtful *either/and* framework with well-reasoned arguments based on clearly stated principles, their point of view could be more rapidly accepted.

Singapore is a good example of a society that has a number of idealistic characteristics. According to Melissa Aratani-Kwee, a Harvard-educated cultural anthropologist, Singapore's government would do well to adopt more *either/and* positions. Policy decisions have often been justified to Singaporeans as necessary sacrifices without which their prosperity would falter. "Either decisive government and order or citizens' free action and chaos, either a highly competitive environment and rapid economic growth or a more relaxed environment and marginal growth." Under such conditions Singaporeans have felt they must settle for the least negative solution as opposed to the most positive one. Aratani-Kwee believes the possibility of creative synergy is often lost in an *either/or* world and proposes a new type of thinking that embraces a more holistic *either/and* point of view.[8]

IBM once ran an extremely astute advertisement that speaks directly to the *either/and* model. The setting is a private beach where a powerful and intimidating CEO is meeting with his long time confidant (LTC). The CEO is feeling the weight of his vast responsibility but is glad to be with someone he can trust.

CEO: *Thanks for coming out.*
              The CEO passes a book.
CEO: *Our consultants say this is the best piece of strategic thinking they've ever done... Ever!*
              Pause.
CEO: *But our IT guys say it's a fantasy, not a strategy. It doesn't take into account our systems, technical stuff... they say it won't work.*
LTC: *And you want to know who's telling you the truth?*
CEO: *Exactly.*
              Pause.
LTC: *Well, there's a rub here Stanley. They both are.*[9]

The commercial goes on to state that in times like this, when confusion reigns, IBM can be of real service. IBM's considerable prowess aside, coming to terms with the *either/and* paradox is a big first step. Then we can begin to replace a "my way or the highway" posture with a more tolerant *either/and* stance.

In summary, idealists can make a valuable contribution to society by signaling when circumstances are badly askew and pointing the way to solutions based on universal principles. Idealists should remember, however, that it is virtually impossible for any person to see the full picture and, therefore, few people have all the necessary facts at their disposal. Since there are multiple paths up every mountain a flexible approach is the most productive. Finally, idealists tend to focus on developing trends a bit ahead of the masses. To be more effective they may have to allow mistakes to unfold, pick up the pieces and then, when most appropriate, engage and educate those ready to listen.

Escapism

According to the dictionary, escapism is the avoidance of reality by the absorption of the mind in an imaginative (often illusionary) situation.[10] One way of escaping reality is to blame others for one's personal troubles. Blame and accusations are an attempt to make others responsible for what one is too guilty to face. When we give this power to others we become dependent on **THEM**. By seeking to avoid personal complicity, we refuse to accept responsibility for any undesirable results.

Conversely, taking responsibility moves one from excuses to solutions. Many integrated steel companies in the U.S., for example, tried to escape responsibility for their problems by blaming cheap foreign imports. They refused to face reality and make the necessary adjustments. The well-documented demise of a large part of America's steel industry—over 30 bankruptcies since 1977—is now well known.[11] Executives at Nucor Corporation, an upstart, innovative steel manufacturer, took the opposite tack and considered the challenge from imports a blessing. They realized that since steel is heavy and importers have to ship their steel across oceans, domestic producers should have a huge competitive advantage. By confronting the situation honestly and realistically they have been able to make the adaptations required and build a strong, sustainable business.[12]

Aratani-Kwee addressed key aspects of self-responsibility when she said,

> The concept of self-responsibility is about knowing and acting from one's authentic self so as to create value... With this awareness, individuals are able to make informed choices that derive from an internal purpose

and motivation. Self-responsibility is a transformative process that builds sustainable partnerships, seeks opportunities, not problems, focuses on the long term but not the short term, involves inclusive adaptability but not exclusive control, and builds trust and overcomes doubt.[13]

Malaysia provides a good example of political escapism. During the 1997 Asian financial crisis, Malaysia looked for scapegoats to avoid responsibility for its ill-conceived economic policies. Here is the background. Eighteen million people occupy a land area of only 127,000 square miles. Prime Minister Mahathir bin Mohamad, intent on showcasing this tiny country, constructed the tallest and longest buildings in the world, an airport with the tallest control tower, a hotel with the tallest flagpole and a $20 billion Multimedia Super Corridor to challenge California's Silicon Valley and its high-tech products. Believing that Malaysia's burgeoning economy required a new capital, Mahathir developed plans for a new $8 billion city that would house 250,000 people. These and other controversial projects required large capital investment and led to large trade deficits. Mahathir insisted that capital inflows were being used for worthwhile long-term projects, not current consumption. Many of the projects were financed by the foreign capital of Investment Vigilantes (IVs) and some of the projects were not economically viable. The IVs did what prudent investors do and hedged their investments, which were denominated in local currency, by selling the Malaysian currency short (selling foreign currency that one does not own in the belief it can be bought in the future at a lower price—thereby making an offsetting profit). Meanwhile, Malaysia's current account deficit approached an alarming 8 percent of GDP. When the roof caved in during the summer of 1997, the Malaysian government looked for someone to blame. IVs, including the world-renowned currency trader George Soros, bore the brunt of the attack. This despite the fact that Malaysia's central bank was also considered a major currency speculator. On September 1, 1998, Mahathir froze Malaysia's rapidly depreciating currency and impounded all foreign investor capital. Needless to say, IVs around the world as well as other participants in the global economy were shocked and outraged.[14] In the eyes of some, Mahathir regained at least part of the respect he lost in 1997–1998 when, in opening remarks made at the World Economic Forum in Davos, Switzerland in 2003, he astutely observed: "We have in fact made a mess of the world... [We are not] much more capable of managing our affairs than Stone Age people."[15]

Nonetheless, Malaysia's capital controls and Argentina's banking freeze remain ominous legacies for developing countries. IVs, who fear their capital can be frozen, will be reluctant to commit funds to foreign countries where economic stability is precarious. Alternatively, IVs build these negative outcomes into their financial equations and insist upon higher returns from emerging markets to compensate for higher risks.

When we try to escape reality by blaming *THEM* for our problems—Argentina: foreign bankers; steel producers: foreign imports; Malaysia: foreign speculators, responsibility is improperly assigned. Power is, thereby, transferred from the blamers to the blamed.

Protectionism

Protectionism is an economic policy designed to insulate domestic industry from foreign competition through restrictions on imports.

One case against protectionism, and in favor of free trade, is based on the fact that unimpeded international trade promotes a mutually profitable division of labor that improves productivity and, thereby, enhances economic growth and living standards of people everywhere. Conversely, imposing tariffs, quotas and duties to protect domestic markets discourages imports and raises prices to consumers. High-cost domestic producers are protected while the economic benefits of the division of labor are obviated.[16]

Protectionism strikes at a core issue, namely, should geographic borders be used to halt transactions that would otherwise take place if both parties were on the same side of the border. In pondering this question it is important to remember that borders are not determined by any higher power and have been changed frequently throughout history. Hermetically sealed borders result in declining standards of living and can diminish the enrichment that comes from cultural exchange.

Politically inspired protectionist policies have engendered international frictions leading to armed conflict. There is an old adage that says: when goods cannot cross borders, armies surely will. While protectionism is based on the opposing interests of nations, free trade connects countries and emphasizes their mutual interests. People involved in cross border commerce are, therefore, more likely to view people from other countries as partners in mutually beneficial cooperative activities. As Thomas G. Palmer, senior fellow at the Cato Institute says: "trade is at the very foundation of human civilization."[17]

Tariffs are one of the least transparent forms of taxation. The effect they have on the price of a product is never clearly identified so consumers do not see what tariffs really cost them. Tariffs are a regressive form of taxation as the rates imposed on necessities, such as food and clothing, are high relative to the rates on luxury items. The EU's Common Agricultural Policy (CAP) is a good example of the counterproductive effects of protectionism. Around $40 billion, half the EU's budget, is distributed every year through the CAP even though farmers account for less than 5 percent of the EU's workforce.[18] With indirect farm subsidies such as price supports and other tax benefits added to these direct payments, EU farmers have received billions of dollars in aid. About 35 percent of the income of the EU farmer is derived from subsidies, compared to 21 percent in the U.S. and just 1 percent in New Zealand. This generosity extracts a heavy price not only from EU consumers but also from citizens in developing countries.[19]

According to estimates by the Organisation For Economic Co-Operation and Development, Europe's protectionist agricultural policies increased the price of food in the EU by 15 percent to 20 percent while farmers in poorer countries are prevented from exporting farm goods to Europe. Because food prices in Europe are far above world levels, surpluses are commonly generated and, aided by even more subsidies, food is then sold to the already suffering developing countries. Since "food security" in Europe ceased to be a substantive issue decades ago, the primary effect of agricultural subsidies is to raise the ire of poor countries and to contribute to the deterioration of the environment through over-farming and the corresponding over-use of chemicals.[20] Many in the EU recognize the foolishness of these protectionist policies and, as a result, the European Commission has made proposals to reform the system. Nonetheless, countries, such as France, that benefit disproportionately from CAP, have been quick to oppose any radical changes without a struggle. What happens in the EU will be a good test of whether common sense can triumph over patently absurd, *ME*-focused, protectionist policies.

Separatism

Separatism is based on the belief that everything (people, animals, trees, rivers, etc.) is composed of isolated, autonomous units that have little if any connection to anything else. This *ME*-focused stance reflects the Newtonian worldview and is based on a mechanistic, subject-object analysis of life. In this model of reality, the universe is a pile of fragments that interact with one another due to outside forces, such as gravity. Taken further, the challenge of life can be seen as navigating through these opposing forces so that our needs can be met with as little discomfort as possible. In other words, we are all on our own and we must become strong enough to secure what we need through the use of physical power, social status, persuasion, political clout or financial influence.[21]

A separatist worldview pits man against man, man against nature and region against region. We have already discussed many of the inhumane, destructive effects the policy of apartheid had on the lives of South African blacks and whites alike. One additional legacy is the effect on South Africa's ecosystem. Legislation enacted in the first half of the 20th century limited black land ownership to 13 percent of the country and required divestiture of community and family lands. This impinged upon the livelihood of countless people. In addition, past "conservation" projects disregarded human rights to such an extent that conservation came to be equated with dispossession. Feelings of alienation and disconnection from the land were common. Consequently, South African blacks see environmental issues as a purely middle-class white concern and are very suspicious of the underlying motives.[22] There is an inexorable link between the long-term vitality of nature and the survival of humanity; failure to recognize this link leads to the adoption of a separative point of view where people exploit natural resources for their personal short-term advantage.

Nationalism is a form of separatism that asserts as primary the interests of one's own nation, as separate from the interests of other nations or the common interests of all nations. Despite the fact that all borders are arbitrary and temporary, nationalists believe their country has superior qualities or attributes. In an effort to preserve and protect their possessions from other regions, separatists have built fences, moats and walls around their community or nation. While in China, I naturally visited the Great Wall and was fascinated by this age-old attempt to protect national borders. A few days later, a university student asked my opinion on the United States' plan to build a missile defense shield around part or all of the country. I replied that, just as the Great Wall was ineffective at keeping people out, the missile defense system would be similarly ineffective. Critics of the plan agree that MDS will not work, that it is exorbitantly expensive, that it will lead to a arms-building competition and that it does nothing to stop the most dangerous threat—terrorism. To quote United States Senator Joseph R. Biden Jr., former chairman of the Senate Foreign Relations Committee, "The administration's obsession with missile defense—with a price tag in excess of a quarter trillion dollars for the layered program on the president's wish list—is doubly troubling because of the attention and resources being diverted from critical efforts to address the genuine threats." According to Senator Biden, the Joint Chiefs of Staff believe an ICBM launch ranks last on the "Threat Spectrum."[23] In addition, if built, the missile defense system is likely to suffer the fate of the last round of offensive missiles; it will ultimately turn to rust and have to be dismantled and destroyed at considerable additional expense. Ed Dunford, retired president of TRW Inc., a large transnational corporation, and former head of its space and defense sector, acknowledged that it is hard to understand why so many (60,000) nuclear warheads were built by the U.S. and Russia. The sad irony is that many of the same aerospace companies have been hired to destroy the exact weapons they helped build.[24]

Contrast this with the unilateral decision of the Bush administration to refrain from participating in the Kyoto Protocol. While tacitly acknowledging the increasingly convincing evidence that global warming is a serious problem, they argue that the Kyoto benefits are not sufficient to justify the costs. This obstinate, go-it-alone stance seriously damages America's influence around the world at a time when the need for global cooperation is growing. The administration approach, which seriously endangers the world ecosystem, is based on the outdated and misguided notion that environmental protection and economic growth are mutually exclusive. History shows that when industries address their environmental problems, they create new technologies that shrink projected costs and increase efficiency and competitive position.

As American taxpayers go shopping, it will be interesting to see how they choose to spend their money. On a missile defense system that is inordinately expensive, probably will not work, is unlikely to be needed, is vehemently opposed by many countries, may lead to new arms buildup and will not deter terrorists? Or on the implementation of the Kyoto Protocol which is widely supported, is likely to be less expensive and more successful than the critics allege, would show America's willingness to restrain its disproportionately large dispersion of greenhouse emissions and thereby encourage other countries to make a greater effort to cooperate on important global issues? The choice is too obvious to dwell on. Saying yes to missile defense systems and no to the environment is a bad deal for American consumers and taxpayers and a source of significant hostility from citizens around the world. In fact, unless these two positions are reversed, U.S. citizens will be agreeing to policies that, although in opposite ways, are based on the indefensible logic of separatism.

Separative thinking, no matter what form it takes, has never worked; in today's quickly shrinking, interdependent world, isolationist and unilateralist policies have even less chance of succeeding.

Terrorism

Terrorism, the use of fear and threats to intimidate, is often fueled by deep-seated resentments against the behaviors described above. There is no justification for heinous acts of terror. Nonetheless, it is important to consider why terrorists feel so desperate that they seek uncivilized, destructive outlets for their fury. Acts of terrorism are triggered, at least in part, when egotism culminates in selfish choices, idealism rejects alternative positions, escapism supplants self-responsibility, protectionism stifles legitimate opportunities and separatism disconnects the life of one person from another.

When those in power exert their might in an egotistic, coercive manner, bitterness builds. Super strength does not assure super wisdom. In the global age cooperation is imperative and being number one in military or economic strength isn't what it once was.

> *Having an empire does not make us safer. The animosity toward the United States of groups and nations in far-flung places—demonstrated graphically by the attacks of September 11th—indicate that imperial overstretch has quite the opposite effect.[25] The resentment of U.S. neo-imperialism could provoke catastrophic terrorism against the United States itself—thereby dramatically reducing U.S. security.[26]*

The disdain of the Bush administration for international agreements has been all too obvious. Almost from the beginning they rejected the Kyoto and anti-ballistic missile treaties, then the International Criminal Court's right to try war crimes and, more recently, they have abdicated international law regarding prisoner rights in Guantanamo and Abu Ghraib. The unilateralist policies of the administration are based on the egotistical premise that they know what is best and everyone must follow their directives. This approach is a clear example of *either/or* thinking. It alienates allies and isolates the unilateralist at a time when terrorist threats require maximum international cooperation. According to Walter Cronkite, "This new self-centered policy found its ultimate—though hardly final—expression when Bush told the U.N. Security Council that the United States was going to invade Iraq, with or without council approval."[27] There is, of course, a price to be paid for arrogantly contrived policies that disregard the views of others. In this case, many believe the terrorist threat is now more resilient and menacing, particularly in Iraq, than would otherwise have been the case.

The problems created by a "you're either with me or against me" approach may be starting to sink in. At an international security conference Donald Rumsfeld, U.S. Secretary of Defense, acknowledged he is not sure if the war against terrorists is being won or lost. Said Rumsfeld, "We need to do even more than simply attempt to capture, kill or thwart terrorists. We have to find ways to persuade young Muslims that the way of the future is through education and opportunity, not through suicide and terrorism."[28]

Egotism displayed by an entrepreneur, a labor leader or a politician, eventually leads to resentment, which, if not mollified, is followed by a rebellious backlash.

Idealism is characterized by passionately held beliefs that motivate behavior toward specific outcomes or results. Idealists, in their most radical manifestation, believe every aspect of life is governed by a single set of ideas, often religious or political in nature. These ideas have few limits or boundaries; any and all means can be used to eliminate opposition and further their cause. Roger Von Oeck pinpointed the fatal flaw in idealism, when he said "There is nothing more dangerous than an idea, when it's the only one you have."[29]

In the eyes of syndicated columnist Crispin Sartwell, suicide bombers are perhaps one of the most cogent examples of idealism run amok. While in no way condoning terrorism, Sartwell uses the oxymoronic term "monstrous saint" to capture the contradictory attributes ascribed to most terrorists. "They yearn to show by a heroic act that they are not merely self-interested and that they are dedicated in the most serious way to helping their people, all people, or the world." Sartwell continues, "Terrorism results from the application of moral heroism to a situation in which constructive action seems impossible or real targets inaccessible."[30]

Henry Ford II addressed the evils of *protectionism* in a 1953 speech:

> *A protectionist trade policy is divisive. It sets a very bad example for others who we have been urging to abandon the restrictive practices that they employ. In the eyes of the world, it is basically isolationist. If we allow the present drift toward economic isolationism to dominate our policies, we will rapidly reach a point where we cannot lead, others will not follow, and the whole fabric of free world cooperation could fall apart at the seams.*[31]

Almost half a century later, General Wesley K. Clark, NATO's former Supreme Allied Commander, had this to say about terrorism,

> *Our best protection is not going to be to build a wall around America. It's not going to be to create a missile defense impenetrable shield. It's going to be, instead, to create a community of common values and shared responsibilities and shared interests in which nations and people get along... It's going to be found in establishing a*

global safety net that starts with security and goes to eco-
nomic development and political development and the
kinds of modernization that let others enjoy the fruits of
modernization that we as Americans enjoy... That really
is ultimately the only protection.[32]

Henry Ford describes the undesirable consequences of a divisive policy of protectionism. General Clark makes the connection between economic progress and the ability to defuse the terrorist threat. Protectionism creates hostility and resentment. Free trade makes prosperity possible.

Shortly after the terrorist attacks on September 11, 2001, U.S. Trade Representative Robert Zoellick asserted that America's trade policies are an integral part of the "counteroffensive" against terrorist aggressors.[33] How does a reduction in trade barriers make a country safer? By giving the world access to domestic markets, either unilaterally or in cooperation with other nations, the message is loud and clear—our interests are best served by helping others prosper. Protectionist tariffs, subsidies and quotas inhibit the ability of the poorest people to export their goods and earn a living. Open market policies promote conditions in which human freedom can flourish. When unemployment rates are far above average, as they are throughout the Muslim world, autocracy and repression thrive. In much of the region, the only way to challenge the status quo is by radical means. As Brink Lindsey states, "Today, a determined policy of market opening can help to reduce the appeal of Islamist extremism—and fear of the American colossus."[34] Free trade is not a cure-all; it often creates temporary dislocations. But when used with sensitivity and discretion, it can be a constructive tool for changing the beliefs, behaviors and conditions that lead to acts of violence. It is increasingly clear that those who feel they cannot share in the prosperity of the world are inevitable targets for the radical thinking that makes terrorism possible. Building fences or walls for the purpose of favoring or protecting a country or region failed in the past. We now live in a borderless world and protectionism of any kind—cultural, economic or military—is doomed to failure.

Escapism leads people to blame others for their plight. Escapists take on the role of victim, choosing accusation and denial over self-responsibility. Often, the blame may be deserved; no conflict is ever completely the fault of one side. Any country that tries to impose its values on others, props up authoritarian regimes for self-serving purposes, consumes a grossly disproportionate amount of natural resources while neglecting its environmental obligations and protects its borders to the detriment of others needs to examine its policies and their effects. Charles Pena, director of defense policy at the Cato Institute, is concerned about the United States' unwillingness to question its own Mideast policies. According to Pena, "This is not a question of blaming America, but it is a question of understanding [that] when we do things in the world there are potential consequences. Until we are willing to engage in that critical self-examination… we're not going to get to the heart of what a lot of the terrorist problem really is."[35]

People who avoid personal responsibility are often passionately devoted to a cause the rightness of which is not subject to debate. They are easily taken in by the opinions of others. Terrorism, along with other forms of mutual destruction, is the inevitable result of the parties refusing to acknowledge their responsibilities for the part they play.

Separatism is the most corrosive of the isms. All isms are related in some fashion to the belief that everything is separate. When we believe we are isolated and autonomous rather than connected and dependent, we might think of ourselves as special or better than others. This leads to behavior that harms others or makes them feel inferior. Resentment and rage builds and can culminate in terrorist actions.

As *The 9/11 Commission Report* concluded, "When people lose hope, when societies break down, when countries fragment, the breeding grounds for terrorism are created."[36] To counteract such dangerous conditions Donald G. Ellis, a fellow at the Asch Center for the Study of Ethnopolitical Conflict at the University of Pennsylvania, recommends a more inclusive foreign policy that respects all cultures and forthrightly addresses the inferiority and humiliation issues.[37] As was evident in the Apartheid era in South Africa, separating people into two classes—privileged versus deprived—inevitably leads to discord and strife.

Countries that engage in protectionist policies only do so when they view the world as separate and disconnected. Countries or individuals seeing the world as connected and interdependent find it difficult to favor one group at the expense of another. Laboring under the illusion of separation, people can escape reality by blaming others and adopting a victim mentality. Outrageous behavior, including terrorist acts that disregard the sanctity of life and the freedom of choice, can then be rationalized. Absent such a view, there is the recognition that thoughts, words and deeds have consequences. In an interdependent world, one accepts responsibility for his or her status or circumstances. Harming others would be seen as harming oneself and, therefore, not reasonable. Those living with a separative point of view often try to impose ideas on others. Such self-righteous, idealistic fervor leads to everything from verbal abuse to armed conflict. A connected, dependent worldview, on the other hand, is directly correlated with a diminution of conflicts.

The preceding chapters have covered many contentious issues that have surfaced as the global economy has become more complex and interdependent. The motivations that underpin these conflicts are an exclusive focus on satisfying *ME* and a need to look for approval from or divert responsibility to *THEM*. *THEM*- and *ME*-focused behavior tends to get translated into a variety of rigid isms. The five discussed in this chapter have been shown to be some of the precursors of terrorism. Understanding the faulty foundation of these beliefs can help one choose a different view of life. In the next chapters we delve into understanding the world in a way that creates an *US* respect for the common good. We also look at examples of successful companies and communities that are implementing this new way of thinking and the transformative benefits that result.

Notes

1. William McDonough and Michael Braungart, *Cradle to Cradle: Remaking the Way We Make Things* (New York: North Point Press, a division of Farrar, Straus and Giroux, 2002), 149.
2. Joseph W. Weiss, *Business Ethics: A Stakeholder and Issues Management Approach,* 2nd ed. (Fort Worth, TX: The Dryden Press—Harcourt Brace College Publishers, 1998), 84–85.
3. Anthony Bianco, William Symonds and Nanette Byrnes, "The Rise and Fall of Dennis Kozlowski," *BusinessWeek,* 23 December 2003, 74.
4. Robin Grugal, "Hold on to Your Ego," *Investor's Business Daily,* 24 May 2002, A3.
5. Weiss, Business Ethics, 85.
6. *Transformation: A Weekly Newsletter for Members of the World Business Academy,* 3 May 1999.
7. "The Green Threat?" *The Economist,* 1 December 2001, 31.
8. Melissa Aratani-Kwee, "Civil Society and the Crafting of Self-Responsibility," in *State-Society Relations in Singapore,* ed. Gillian Koh and Ooi Goik Ling (Singapore: Oxford University Press, 2000), 222.
9. *The Advisor,* script of a television commercial (IBM Brand Advertising, 2001).
10. *The Random House Dictionary of the English Language,* The Unabridged Edition (New York: Random House, 1967), 486.
11. "A Miracle at Bethlehem," *The Economist,* 11 January 2003, 55.
12. Robin Grugal, "Avoid the Blame Game," *Investor's Business Daily,* 4 July 2002, A3.
13. Aratani-Kwee, "Civil Society and the Crafting of," 224.
14. David F. DeRosa, *In Defense of Free Capital Markets: The Case Against a New International Financial Architecture* (Princeton, NJ: Bloomberg Press, 2001), 107–111.

[15] Mahathir Mohamad, "Trust and Governance for a New Era," *Opening Remarks at the World Economic Forum, Davos, Switzerland, http://www. smpke.jpm.my/webnotesapp/pmmain.nsf*: 23 January 2003.

[16] Paul A. Samuelson, *Economics: An Introductory Analysis,* Sixth Edition (New York: McGraw-Hill Book Company, 1964), 684.

[17] Tom G. Palmer, "Globalization Is Grrrreat!" *Cato's Letter: A Quarterly Message on Liberty,* 1 (Fall 2002): 5.

[18] "Cleansing the Augean Stables," *The Economist,* 13 July 2002, 12.

[19] "Will These Modest Proposals Provoke Mayhem Down on the Farm?" *The Economist,* 13 July 2002, 42.

[20] Ibid.

[21] Denise Breton and Christopher Largent, *The Paradigm Conspiracy: How Our Systems of Government, Church, School and Culture Violate Our Human Potential* (Center City, MN: Hazelden, 1996), 258.

[22] Jacklyn Cock and Alison Bernstein, *Melting Pots & Rainbow Nations: Conversations About Difference in the United States and South Africa* (Urbana, IL: University of Illinois Press, 2002), 74.

[23] Joseph R. Biden, Jr., "Missile Defense Delusion," *The Washington Post,* 19 December 2001, A39.

[24] Peter Benesh, "How Sept. 11 Brought Russia, U.S. Together," *Investor's Business Daily,* 18 October 2001, A5.

[25] Ivan Eland, "The Empire Strikes Out: The 'New Imperialism' and Its Fatal Flaws," *Cato Institute Policy Analysis,* 459 (26 November 2002), 21.

[26] Ibid., 18.

[27] Walter Cronkite, "American Unilateralism Alienates Allies, Isolates Us," *The Philadelphia Inquirer,* 24 November 2003, A15.

[28] "Rumsfeld: Source of Terrorism May be Growing," *The Philadelphia Inquirer,* 6 June 2004, A5.

[29] Roger Von Oeck, "A Whack on the Side of Your Head," *Copleman Meeting Place: Resources, http://www.earthdreams.net*: 5 May 2002.

[30] Crispin Sartwell, "Terrorism: A Monstrous Sainthood," *The Philadelphia Inquirer,* 31 March 2004, A13.

[31] Henry Ford II, "Expanded Trade and World Peace," An address delivered to the Committee for a National Trade Policy (New York: 26 October 1953).

[32] Robert Moran, "Clark Says U.S. Must Lead Global Change," *The Philadelphia Inquirer,* 18 October 2001, A22.

[33] Robert B. Zoellick, "Countering Terror with Trade," *The Washington Post,* 20 September 2001, A35.

[34] Brink Lindsey, "The Trade Front: Combating Terrorism with Open Markets," *Center for Trade Policy Studies, No. 24* (Cato Institute, 5 August 2003), 14.

[35] "Attention Turns to 9/11 Panel's Recommendations," *Investor's Business Daily,* 23 July 2004, A1.

[36] National Commission on Terrorist Attacks Upon the United States, *The 9/11 Commission Report* (New York: W.W. Norton & Company, 2004), 378.

[37] Donald G. Ellis, "Terrorists Aren't 'Crazy'," *The Philadelphia Inquirer,* 3 September 2003, A13.

Chapter Nine

Self-interestStretching

Earlier chapters have demonstrated our unavoidable exposure to the distorted, often immature views of many world leaders and authority figures. The isms cited in the previous chapters—egotism, idealism, protectionism, escapism and separatism—are endemic to all cultures and geographic regions. The globalization process depends on trust and cooperation to function properly; it is seriously jeopardized by uninformed decision-makers wedded to erroneous, divisive beliefs. How can this process, that should be unifying and beneficial, be revitalized to achieve its potential and gain broad support? Specifically, "What is the source of our problems?"

Many observers believe that conflicts are due to tensions and resentments that naturally arise when some people are thriving while others are failing. People who are well educated, financially sophisticated and/or technologically skilled have generally been able to prosper; those who are not may suffer, sometimes severely. As long as the benefits of economic production go primarily to a limited group, conflicts between the "haves" and "have-nots" are inevitable. The root cause, however, goes deeper. It can be directly traced to a difference in worldviews; those who behave in accord with our intimate connectedness—**US**-oriented—and those who see the world as a collection of separate and autonomous parts—**ME**- or **THEM**-focused. The latter two groups believe that the duality they observe daily—hot and cold, up and down, hungry and satiated, solid and liquid, rich and poor, educated and illiterate—is evidence of an *either/or* world of discrete, independent objects and conditions.

Philosophers have long held that all apparent opposites constitute a complementary relationship, in which each of the two poles is dynamically linked to the other. Whereas heat and cold seem to be opposite conditions they are merely varying degrees of the same thing. A solid, such as a block of ice, can easily be transformed into a liquid (water) or a gas (steam) by a change in temperature. What we consider hard and distinct—ice—is just one of many possible forms, any one of which can manifest almost instantaneously. The same concept can be applied to emotions. Love and hate, for instance, can blend into each other so that it becomes impossible to differentiate between them. While on one level it is eminently practical to acknowledge the apparent individuality of things, we must remain acutely aware that all differences are relative and part of an all-encompassing whole. Many of the problems discussed in previous chapters have arisen from the failure to recognize the unity of seemingly separate forms.

Because of this misunderstanding, most of us fall into the **ME** or **THEM** category a majority of the time. Life then becomes a win/lose confrontation based on the belief that vigorously competing for scarce resources is a prerequisite for survival. The notion that others are out to take advantage of us becomes a self-fulfilling prophecy. We believe there is no reason to cooperate with those who will not sacrifice personal short-term gain for mutual long-term benefits. The real problem is not, therefore, the gap between the rich and poor as much as the gap in understanding or, more precisely, in our consciousness. This gap in conscious awareness produces belief systems that engender incompatible concepts of self-interest. As long as we are unaware of this fundamental problem, we can expect everything from contentious behavior to unconscionable acts of terror to be commonplace.

Many executives of companies whose stock collapsed in recent years claimed they were unaware of any pending crisis. *Investor's Business Daily,* a newspaper targeting hardheaded businesspeople, reported that Steve Case, the former chairman of AOL Time Warner, was quoted as saying accounting problems at AOL aren't his doing since he wasn't AWARE of accounting details.[1] *BusinessWeek* ran an article with the subtitle: "Peregrine's (a large software company) chairman says he wasn't AWARE of any financial irregularities. But he cashed out."[2] And in reporting Jeffrey Skilling's Congressional testimony, the *Philadelphia Inquirer* posted the following headline, "Ex-Enron CEO: 'I was not AWARE...'"[3] [Emphasis added] Even if these three statements are true, the lack of awareness on the part of these executives is what led to the problems at their companies. On a larger scale, being unaware of the consequences of everything we think, say and do can be just as destructive.

Animate or Inanimate—That is the Question

Dr. Margaret Wheatley, best-selling author and consultant to a variety of Fortune 500 clients, believes that the traditional vision of the world as a huge machine prompts us to treat everything as foreign and separate from ourselves. This misperception leads to seeing boundaries between us and others and creates a sense of alienation and the need to dominate and control. It also affects our perception and interpretation of our experiences. We have believed for so long in this mechanistic universe that it is difficult to change focus; to relinquish our concrete, linear view in favor of seeing a network of living systems.[4] The more fluid view of reality helps us understand that organisms are not separate; they are vital threads in an exquisite, unending tapestry.

The level of social advancement can be deduced by examining the extent to which duality thinking prevails. Insistence on making comparisons and characterizing things as better or worse, higher or lower is clear evidence of a separatist worldview. When a society believes in the interrelatedness of all things, conduct that opposes the common good is seen as counterproductive and quickly reversed. Cooperation and sharing become the norm, not for altruistic reasons, but because such behavior is more effective and mutually advantageous than confrontation and hoarding. Living with our fellow inhabitants in a cooperative, supportive manner is infinitely more functional and satisfying.

The Republic of Iceland offers an excellent illustration of how a country of cooperative, supportive citizens built a society where both financial success and personal satisfaction prevail. Iceland generally ranks in the top tier in GDP per capita, in life expectancy, in the Economist's Quality of Life Index, in the Index of Economic Freedom and in the World Competitiveness Survey. Icelanders combine a strong sense of individuality with a keen desire for community. According to Olafur Ragnar Grimsson, Iceland's President, "If you ask Icelanders, 'Who are you?' they will give you an answer that tells you who they are as individuals but at the same time expresses who they are as Icelanders. They never see themselves in isolation from others. They always see themselves as part of a whole... So it was a combination of what we would call today an entrepreneurial spirit in each and everyone as well as a cooperative culture where everyone saw it to his advantage to benefit from the progress of others."[5]

When uncooperative, uncaring attitudes prevail, the social fabric unravels. Increased crime, terrorism and political instability as well as feelings of defiance and despair are likely to follow. In a speech prior to assuming his current position, Robert B. Zoellick, the U. S. Trade Representative in the Bush administration stated: "The failure to supply food, medicine, or basic needs leads to a general breakdown in a society. Such situations involve much more than preserving legal and policy structures; they involve the basic conditions necessary for social order and individual liberty. The potential breakdown threatens the sense of **common good** [emphasis added] upon which all other institutions—including government and business—are built."[6]

More Likes Less Dislikes

Capitalism rests on the premise that human beings are rational creatures motivated to act for perceived benefits. Yet most of our actions serve the *ME* and *THEM* part of our personality. Thus, self-interest seems to be centered on acquisitive behavior, where the consumption of goods and services often reaches insatiable levels. Well-known Chilean economist, Manfred Max-Neef, believes efficiency, speed of production and the proliferation of goods and services have become ends in themselves and do little to satisfy our fundamental needs. People have become increasingly dependent on the system of production while, at the same time, more alienated from the system and its consequences. Our quality of life is overshadowed by the compulsion to enhance productivity and, thereby, increase economic growth. This helps to explain why many people who have worked hard and achieved what they were taught were worthy, fulfilling goals often feel dissatisfied with their lives. A society that equates self-interest with the needs of all of *US*, on the other hand, provides its citizens with more of what they really want—flourishing, healthy, safe, attractive communities and less of what they abhor—pollution, violence, crime and the attendant emotional stress.

The Golden Rule, which defines self-interest in the broadest, most inclusive terms, is probably the most universally accepted prescription for leading an exemplary life. The Golden Rule is not merely a lofty ideal devoid of everyday practicality. *Investor's Business Daily* featured a long-running series entitled Leaders and Success. The series highlighted a surprisingly large number of entrepreneurs and business executives who attribute their success to company-wide implementation of the Golden Rule. The founders of J.C. Penney and Southwest Airlines are two of the best-known CEOs that used this age-old maxim as the guiding principle for their business dealings. (Variations of the Golden Rule as articulated by many cultures throughout the centuries are detailed at the end of the chapter).

How can we reconcile the predominance of today's selfish, separative worldview with the all-inclusive, common-good orientation espoused by the most revered teachers? I have had success resolving this dilemma for thousands of businesspeople in presentations given throughout the United States. First, it is necessary to recognize the extent to which we have been conditioned to rely on our senses to reveal what is going on in the world. For most of us seeing is believing; anything not seen is dismissed as worthless. Second, consider how often our senses are misleading or inaccurate. As an example, our eyes disclose a world that looks flat and a sun that appears to revolve around the earth. Stars that have collapsed into black holes mistakenly appear to be intact and active due to the length of time it takes light to reach our planet. And we are all familiar with optical illusions and the fact that two people can view the same picture and report seeing two entirely different objects.

What we see is not only a function of our eyesight but of the way our brain interprets these sensory images. Our interpretations are based on our previous experiences. In a scientific experiment, optical illusions created with lines and edges were shown to two different African tribes. The tribe that had little contact with advanced technology saw through the illusion; the other tribe did not. The explanation—the first tribe lived in round houses with curved edges and rarely saw anything with a right angle.

One of the most common optical illusions is the "moving picture" shown on television and in movie theaters; we see these images as moving despite the fact that we know they are only a series of still pictures. Humans are able to perceive only a minute fraction of the available sound and light spectrum. Tying our view of reality to our senses is exceedingly limiting. Einstein made this clear when he stated: "Up to the 20th century, reality was everything humans could touch, smell, see, and hear. Since the initial publication of the chart of the electromagnetic spectrum, humans have learned that what they can touch, smell, see and hear is less than one millionth of reality."[7]

Sense and NonSense

If our senses are not as informative as we have been led to believe, what is it we do not see? Physicists tell us that everything that exists is composed of energy. This energy has consciousness and is in constant motion. The cells of our bodies are composed of these energy packets and they ceaselessly travel throughout the cosmos. And it is not only physical objects that are filled with this conscious energy but the space between objects as well. Thus, we are profoundly connected to every part of the universe. As Einstein protégé David Bohm stated, "The inseparable quantum interconnectedness of the whole universe is the fundamental reality."[8]

Thoughts are as real and enduring as any physical object. An unkind statement about someone, whether actually spoken or merely thought, can have real, consequential effects. Erwin Schrodinger, well-known quantum physicist, reinforced this idea when he said, "Mind by its very nature is a *singulare tantum*... the overall number of minds is just one."[9] This view of the world depicts the underlying unity that exists slightly beyond the confines of our physical senses. Until our beliefs and behaviors are based on a more holistic view of reality, the conflicts described in Part Two will continue to haunt us.

Thought Shifting

Staying conscious of our interconnectedness is a crucial first step in moving toward an *US*-dominant point of reference. With this objective in mind, let's examine some of today's entrenched beliefs:

- The poor and disadvantaged are not my concern.
- Unethical behavior is necessary to compete successfully.
- If natural resources were more equitably shared there wouldn't be enough for me.
- Contributing to society and making money are mutually exclusive.
- Investors in a company will suffer if all stakeholders are given equal consideration.
- Protectionist policies benefit the citizens of the country.
- Economic growth will cure all ills.
- Policies that ensure environmental vitality inhibit economic growth.

A cursory examination of these beliefs is sufficient to uncover their obvious flaws. The last two statements in particular are the basis of many mistaken public policy decisions and, as such, deserve further scrutiny.

The World Bank's annual World Development Report (WDR) asserts that economic growth alone is not sufficient to alleviate poverty and improve environmental conditions. Sustainable development requires not only an increase in net worth but an improvement in individual feelings of self-worth. In order to further economic growth and avoid civil unrest, the poor and disenfranchised must have greater access to both physical (land, labor and capital) and social (property rights, the rule of law and full and unobstructed transparency) assets. In many countries, powerful individuals in government and business appropriate an inordinate amount of these assets. This results in the benefits, even of otherwise prudent policies, being enjoyed by a relative few while the costs are widely dispersed and, therefore, fall disproportionately on those who can least afford them.[10] Creating a more satisfying and sustainable life requires that we rethink the "growth at any price" paradigm and institute an approach that takes account of all participants and all conceivable consequences.

Let us now probe the widely held *either/or* view that claims economic growth and responsible environmental stewardship are incompatible. A review of environmental legislation over the last few decades provides perspective on the separative arguments put forth by those with an ax to grind. The American Automobile Manufacturers Association, representative of this self-serving type of thinking, staunchly opposed the U.S. Clean Air Act of 1970. The Association vociferously maintained that implementation of these standards would compel the industry to shut down. In 1974, an industry executive testified before a Senate committee that new fuel economy standards would force the industry to limit production to sub-compact cars. (Anyone else notice the proliferation of SUVs on the highway?) During the 1990 Clean Air Act debate, automobile executives claimed that it would be financially ruinous if they had to reduce auto emissions. Despite this warning, the U.S. enacted new laws that demanded a 39 percent reduction in hydrocarbons and a 60 percent reduction in nitrogen oxides in car emissions. Years of impressive auto manufacturing profits followed.[11]

People are creatures of habit; changing behavior is excruciatingly difficult. Having struggled to modify my own behavior for many years, I can certainly attest to the ongoing challenges. The need for stability coupled with the fear of the unknown often keeps us paralyzed. Maintaining the status quo seems safer even in the face of compelling evidence to the contrary. Only when brought face to face with irrefutable danger—a dramatic increase in skin cancers or an accelerated melting of glaciers that forces rivers to overflow—do we make the necessary changes. Meaningful transformations require the courage to re-examine our beliefs and broaden our understanding of self-interest. Here are some steps that will help facilitate a major shift in thinking. The first two steps are covered in this chapter; the last three will be discussed in the ensuing chapters.

1. Become aware of the widely held belief that all things are discrete and unrelated and notice the counterproductive nature of this view.
2. Analyze the distribution of your *ME-*, *THEM-* and *US-*motivations, how they affect your thoughts and actions and observe whether they are aligned with universal principles of equality and justice.
3. Choose your priorities and values so they conform to the highest stage of moral development and level of need currently possible.

4. Engage with and educate others about the practical benefits and sense of fulfillment that accompanies an *US*-orientation.

5. If your unconventional ideas are ridiculed or rejected by status quo traditionalists, take comfort in what others (Mother Teresa, Mahatma Gandhi and Albert Schweitzer) have accomplished by acting for the common good and serving all of *US*.

This chapter has made the case that the world is far more connected and dependent than our physical senses reveal. Our most revered teachers have articulated this interdependent view of life for thousands of years. More recently many esteemed scientists have echoed these sentiments. Many of us accept it on an intellectual level. The next step is to incorporate this idea into what we say and how we act. We need to recognize that behavior is directly influenced by our concept of self-interest. Are we best served by 1) satisfying our immediate, exclusive needs or by 2) looking to others to gain acceptance or transfer blame, or by 3) doing what is best for all concerned? At times, we all respond to each of these three voices. It is important to learn how our responses are distributed among these three alternatives and which motivation usually prevails. Unless we are aware of our tendencies, we can't consciously choose to change them. It takes courage and persistence to act in opposition to what we have been taught. Honest self-examination is both challenging and liberating. Changing habitual patterns is best accomplished in small, organic increments and with acceptance of those parts of us that are less than perfect. It is difficult, if not impossible, to do this work alone; a few books that discuss these issues and organizations that specialize in this work are listed later in the chapter. To the extent we become *US*-dominant—living the golden rule and acting for the common good—we move closer to self-realization and an enhanced sense of self-worth and well-being.

The two self-assessment questionnaires that follow were designed to help readers determine their dominant motivations. They have been given to people with a variety of educational, cultural and economic backgrounds. The first one refers to situations described in the previous chapters and asks readers to consider what choices they might have made under similar circumstances. The second is not as specific. It scrutinizes our everyday needs, desires, values and idiosyncrasies. The questionnaire is offered to assist in our search for self-knowledge. The better we understand ourselves, the easier it is to modify our behavior and this, in turn, will encourage others to follow suit. As Mahatma Gandhi said, "You must be the change you wish to see in the world."

Self-Assessment Questionnaire I

Please respond to each statement by using the following scale:

1. Strongly disagree
2. Mildly disagree
3. Neutral; no opinion
4. Mildly agree
5. Strongly agree

_____ A. Argentines are right to hold the IMF responsible for their economic problems.

_____ B. People in developing countries who lose their jobs have every right to blame the globalization process for their misfortune.

_____ C. If I were imprisoned under the same circumstances as Nelson Mandela, I believe I would be able to forgive my captors.

_____ D. I am willing to pay more for recycled material because it is better for the environment.

_____ E. I would be willing to forego current government subsidies that are advantageous to my business if I thought it was best for the overall economy.

_____ F. CEOs work long and hard under pressure-packed conditions and are, therefore, entitled to receive compensation that may be several hundred times what their employees earn.

_____ G. If my success depends on obtaining a large order, which can only be won by bribing a government official, I'd be willing to do so.

_____ H. Once past middle age I will let my children and grandchildren make the life-style adjustments needed to protect the environment; I expect to be too set in my ways to change.

_____ I.   The U.S. steel industry is the victim of ineffective government policies and unfair foreign competition.

Tabulating the questionnaire:

Add up the score (1–5) for each set of letters and place on the line to the right.

F, G, and H	A. _____
A, B, and I	B. _____
C, D, and E	C. _____

All of us have a part of ourselves that is {A} primarily interested in our narrow self-interest {B} concerned about how we are perceived by others and/or blame others for unfavorable circumstances, and {C} connected to the whole and focused on the common good.

Are you surprised at the relative strength of these three parts as indicated by the score attributed to A, B and C?
Yes _____   No _____

The second questionnaire may prove more revealing. Fearless honesty and genuine self-acceptance are recommended.

Self-Assessment Questionnaire II

Please respond to each statement by using the following scale:

1. Strongly disagree
2. Mildly disagree
3. Neutral; no opinion
4. Mildly agree
5. Strongly agree

_____ A.   I get upset if circumstances and events aren't exactly the way I think they should be.

_____ B.   I am concerned about making a mistake in front of others.

_____ C.   I never worry about the future or regret the past.

_____ D.   Sometimes it is okay to cut corners or exaggerate the truth if it helps me get what I want.

_____ E.   I often feel like I am the victim of an unfair world.

_____ F.   I trust that whatever happens in my life will be for the best.

_____ G.   I am envious when others have something that I want but don't have.

_____ H.   I often judge how others behave.

_____ I.   I am not interested in trying to control people or events.

_____ J.   I prefer the status quo to new conditions or circumstances.

_____ K.   I am concerned about what others think of me.

_____ L.   I trust my intuition completely when making important decisions.

_____ M. My friends sometimes think I am selfish but I am only doing what any rational person would do—act in his/her own self-interest.

_____ N. I am secretive and fear that others will see my unattractive traits.

_____ O. I spend more time considering long-term consequences than short-term results.

_____ P. Until the social needs of my community and country are fully met, making charitable contributions to causes in other countries is a very low priority.

_____ Q. When trying to get others to do something I will often tell them what they want to hear.

_____ R. I seriously consider how everyone may be affected before making decisions.

_____ S. In the long run we are all dead so live it up and don't worry about tomorrow.

_____ T. My well-being is often dependent on the action of others.

_____ U. Once my basic needs are satisfied, all I really want is the pleasure that comes from loving relationships and fulfilling experiences.

Tabulating the questionnaire:

Add up the score (1–5) for each set of letters and place on the line to the right

A, D, G, J, M, P, and S	A. _____
B, E, H, K, N, Q, and T	B. _____
C, F, I, L, O, R, and U	C. _____

All of us have a part of ourselves that is {A} primarily interested in our narrow self-interest, {B} concerned about how we are perceived by others and/or blame others for unfavorable circumstances, and {C} connected to the whole and focused on the common good.

Are you surprised at the relative strength of these three parts as indicated by the score attributed to A, B and C?
Yes _____   No _____

As a result of taking this questionnaire, do you think you may be more aware of the influence the three parts play in your everyday decision-making?
Much more aware _____
Moderately more aware _____
No more aware _____

There are a number of resources available for those who desire to make their thoughts and actions more **US**-focused. For a partial list of material and programs providing assistance, please refer to the following page.

Programs and Resources for Personal and Organizational Transformation

Pathwork International—The Pathwork is a body of material that provides profound insights into our multi-dimensional personality. These insights challenge us to become aware of our illusions so we see the current situation accurately and envision what is possible with the aid of personal development. This is a path of growing self-knowledge and self-acceptance, which leads to self-transformation. *www.pathwork.org*

The Undefended Self—Susan Thesenga, Pathwork Press, 2001.

Richard Barrett and Associates—Provides consultants, change agents and human resource professionals with tools and techniques for assessing their values and implementing organizational transformation. *www.corptools.com*

Liberating the Corporate Soul—Richard Barrett, Butterworth-Heinemann, 1998.

Appreciative Inquiry (AI)—Offers an approach for achieving personal development, organizational change and global transformation. Grounded in affirmation and appreciation, AI shifts the focus from deficit-based change that emphasizes problems to positive change that accentuates constructive possibilities. AI encourages individuals and organizations to see and support the best in others thereby generating high levels of cooperation and innovation. *www.appreciative-inquiry.org*

The Power of Appreciative Inquiry—Diana Whitney & Amanda Trosten-Bloom, Berrett-Koehler, 2003.

BigPictureSmallWorld (BPSW)—Through interactive assemblies, teacher training, books and curriculum material BPSW informs people about global wonders and challenges and motivates them to participate in shaping the world to match their values. *www.bigpicturesmallworld.com*

Global Inc: An Atlas of the Multinational Corporation—Medard Gable and Henry Bruner, New Press, 2003.

The Power of Full Engagement—Jim Loehr & Tony Schwartz, Free Press, 2003. Presents a detailed roadmap that helps people become more physically energized, emotionally connected, mentally focused and spiritually aligned. *www. thepoweroffullengagement.com*

Seven Languages for Transformation—Robert Kegan & Lisa Laskow Lahey, Jossey-Bass, 2001. Provides a practical approach ("new technology") to explain and resolve the complex problem of why, despite genuine aspirations for change, there is so little lasting change actually occurring on either the individual or organizational level.

The Golden Rule

Buddhism: Hurt not others in ways that you yourself would find hurtful. *Udana-Varga, 5:18, 6th Century BCE*

Christianity: Whatsoever ye would that men should do to you, do ye even so to them. *Matthew 7:12, 1st Century CE*

Classical Paganism: May I do to others as I would they should do unto me. *Plato, 4th Century BCE*

Confucianism: Do not unto others what you would not have them do to you. *Analects, 15:23, 6th Century BCE*

Hinduism: Do naught unto others which would cause you pain if done to you. *Mahabharata 5:1517, 3rd Century BCE*

Bah'ai: Lay not on any soul a load which ye would not wish to be laid upon you and desire not for anyone the things you would not desire for yourself. *Baha'u'llah, 19th Century CE*

Islam: No one of you is a believer until he desires for his brother what he desires for himself. *Muhammad, Sunnab, 6th Century CE*

Jainism: In happiness and suffering, in joy and grief, we should regard all creatures as we regard our own self, and should therefore refrain from inflicting upon others such injury as would appear undesirable to us if inflicted upon ourselves. *Lord Mahavir, 24th Tirthankara, 5th Century, BCE*

Judaism: What is hateful to you, do not to your fellow man. *Talmud, Shabbat 31a*

Native American: Do not condemn your brother until you have walked a mile in his moccasins. *Unknown*

Sikhism: Don't create enmity with anyone as God is within everyone. *Guru Arjan Devji 259, Guru Granth Shaib*

Taoism: Regard your neighbor's gain as your own gain and regard your neighbor's loss as your own loss. *Unknown*

Zoroastrianism: Do not do unto others all that which is not well for oneself. *Dadistan-I-Dinik, 94:5, 5th Century BCE*

Notes

1 Doug Tsuruoka, "Case Closed? Accounting Probe May be End for AOL Chairman," *Investor's Business Daily,* 9 October 2002, A1.
2 Arlene Weintraub, "Just How Much Did John Moores Know?" *BusinessWeek,* 14 October 2002, 47.
3 Chris Mondics and Dave Montgomery, "Ex-Enron CEO: 'I Was Not Aware.' " *The Philadelphia Inquirer,* 8 February 2002.
4 Lauren Johnson, "Organizations as Living Systems," review of *A Simpler Way,* by Margaret Wheatley and Myron Kellner-Rogers, *The Systems Thinker,* December 1996/January 1997, 9–11.
5 Larry C. Farrell, *The Entrepreneurial Age: Awakening the Spirit of Enterprise in People, Companies, and Countries* (New York: Allworth Press, an imprint of Allworth Communications, 2001), 243, 245.
6 Robert B. Zoellick, "Strategic Philanthropy for Business," keynote address before the Business-Humanitarian Forum, (Geneva, Switzerland: 27 January 1999).
7 Thomas Claire, *Body Work: What Type of Massage to Get—and How to Make the Most of It* (New York: William Morrow and Company, Inc., 1995), 247.
8 D. Bohm and B. Hiley, "On the Intuitive Understanding of Nonlocality as Implied by Quantum Theory," *Foundations of Physics 5,* (1975): 102.
9 Larry Dossey, M.D., *Healing Words: The Power of Prayer and the Practice of Medicine* (San Francisco: HarperSanFrancisco, 1993), 43.
10 "Sustaining Hope," *The Economist,* 24 August 2002, 56.
11 Krupp, Fred, "Cars Can Get Much Cleaner," *The New York Times,* 20 July 2002.

PART FOUR

THE POSSIBILITIES

"Not everything that counts can be counted, and not everything that can be counted counts."

ALBERT EINSTEIN

Chapter Ten

ValuesOrdering

In EntrepreneurCelebs we saw how some business executives value personal wealth over the interests of other stakeholders—employees, customers, stockholders and the community. EcoIdealists presented examples of how an *either/or* view of life leads some to value economic growth at the expense of environmental sustainability and others to blame capitalism for the degradation of our resources. PoliticalShortimers are notorious for valuing political expediency even when it results in negative long-term consequences. The connection among these is a poor choice of values; values which lead to a narrow and distorted view of self-interest. What is needed is a set of values that promotes harmony with nature and reflects our connection to and responsibility for all of humanity. In this book such values are referred to as "soul values." We embrace them as we develop an increasingly inclusive definition of self-interest.

Later in this chapter, we will look at examples of activities and organizations that pursue these values. First, we need to look at what values are and how we choose among them.

Valuing all of *US*

Values are ideals used to guide individual thoughts and behavior. They are rules for living that indicate a preference for a particular result and provide a structure within which members of a community operate in a responsible, accountable and cohesive manner. Our personal values evolve over time and determine how we interact with and transform the society in which we live. They determine how we relate to one another and to the rest of the world. Many people are unaware of the values that motivate their behavior; they simply act in robot-like fashion programmed by their early conditioning and life experiences. Our values reflect our understanding of life. Who are we and what are we here to do? Are we disconnected and autonomous beings or are we connected and dependent entities with fortunes unalterably linked to the whole? Changing how we think—what we value—is much more powerful than changing external conditions. As we reorient our thinking and take responsibility for our choices we make significant changes in our personal and organizational relationships.[1]

Ideals We Live By

Values are linked to our concept of self-interest and can be divided into three broad categories. The first category includes those values related to our survival (*ME*-focused). Basic needs that affect our health and safety are characteristic of survival values. A person whose attention is concentrated on Maslow's first two levels of need would fall into this category and would likely focus on control, vigilance and receiving or hoarding. Those on the second two levels of

Maslow's hierarchy may embrace one of the two ways *THEM*-focused values can be distorted. In one, appearance is highly prized and emphasis is placed on getting the approval of others or of attaining fame or fortune in order to prove one's worth. The other is characterized by a victim mentality; constantly blaming others instead of taking responsibility for ourselves. The third category—soul values—corresponds to Maslow's fifth level of need (*US*-focused). Sharing generously, creating constructively and serving the common good are the type of attitudes and behavior that are stressed. The foregoing descriptions notwithstanding, values fall on a continuum and, to a greater or lesser degree, people are a composite of survival, appearance and soul values. As we become more aware of the connections among us, the higher-level values begin to play a larger role in our thoughts and actions. These concepts, along with others discussed in previous chapters are summarized in the Matrix of Possibilities displayed on the next page.

Our choice of values is related to the extent to which we are *ME*-, *THEM*- or *US*-dominant. The better we understand our motivations, the more likely we are to make better value choices. All of us, except for the rare individual whose life is totally devoted to serving others, exhibit *ME*- or *THEM*-oriented characteristics. A life focused on *ME* or *THEM* is based on fear—fear that we will not get what we want or fear that we will not please others. It is, therefore, separative in nature and keeps us from developing our fullest potential. If we are honest with ourselves, we will recognize that these fears keep us from attaining joy, meaning and fulfillment. We realize that we must examine our motives; Do we act out of love or fear, unity or separateness? Do we want the false comfort that comes from maintaining the status quo or the fulfilling challenge of self-development? If we choose the latter, our tendency to seek self-esteem from external

MATRIX OF POSSIBILITIES

Level Of Need	Physical	Social	Spiritual
Stage Of Moral Development	Seek Pleasure Avoid Pain	Seek Approval Deflect Responsibility	Seek Self-Knowledge Develop Spiritually
Motivation	ME	THEM	US
Focus	Competing Excluding	Giving Power to Others	Serving Including
Values	Survival *Having* Food Clothing Shelter Safety	Appearance *Doing (as others)* Believe Behave Desire Insist	Soul *Being* Holistically Creative Either/And Tolerant Compassionately Generous Fearlessly Honest

sources diminishes. We begin to accept our circumstances realistically and responsibly rather than blaming others. Humility replaces hubris as we see how our accomplishments are quite often related to forces outside our direct control. We develop a sense of trust that enables us to change priorities and choose values more aligned with universal principles.[2] The examples that follow are illustrative of activities that reflect soul values—creating holistically, giving generously, engaging tolerantly and proclaiming humbly. They correspond, respectively, to our four levels of being—physical, emotional, mental and spiritual. When we create according to the laws of nature, share with those in need and engage diverse groups to transform counterproductive behavior, life becomes more meaningful and fulfilling. Incorporating soul values into all we do raises the overall level of consciousness and makes it possible to move to an *US*-dominant point of view.

Creating *US*

> *We must draw our standards from the natural world.*
> *We must honor with the humility of the wise the bounds*
> *of that natural world and the mystery which lies beyond*
> *them, admitting that there is something in the order of*
> *being which evidently exceeds all our competence.*
>
> *Vaclav Havel,*
> *Former President of the Czech Republic*[3]

Each of us is a creative force; it is the nature of our being. The results of our creativity are sometimes quite simple, at other times more elaborate. A recent example of human ingenuity is the Industrial Revolution where new technology coupled with the discovery of large fossil fuel supplies greatly enhanced human productive capabilities. But all human creations are subject to error and require adjustment; that is how we learn and evolve. One of the unintended consequences of the Industrial Revolution has been a major disconnect between man and nature.[4] It is certainly not in our interest for the benefits of our creativity to be annulled by polluting the ecosystem.

According to McDonough and Braungart's *Cradle to Cradle,* "of the approximately 8000 defined chemical substances and technical mixes produced and used by industries today, only about 3000 have been studied for their effects on living systems." The waste, pollution and harmful products currently produced are not necessarily the result of people doing something morally wrong. "They are the consequence of outdated and unintelligent design."[5] The industrial world has been using an outmoded "cradle to grave" model, wherein more than 90 percent of the material used to make durable goods becomes hard-to-dispose-of waste products almost immediately.[6] In addition, many products are designed with "built-in obsolescence" encouraging the consumer to discard a perfectly serviceable product and buy a new version.

Doing more with less is the goal of the currently popular "eco-efficiency" model. Reuse and regulation are the means used to achieve this end. This is, however, an incomplete model. Merely reducing the quantity of raw materials used for a product or the toxic waste resulting from its dematerialization does not halt environmental depletion and destruction—it only slows them down.[7] The current eco-efficiency model is valuable as a transitional step but is limited because it works within the same system that caused the problem to begin with. What is needed is a change in perspective from needing to control nature to working in coordination with it. Modern industrial design consists in pushing away, shutting out and attempting to control unevenly distributed natural abundance. We rarely if ever question this model; we assume that, if we haven't been able to achieve the desired result, we are not trying hard enough.[8]

McDonough Braungart Design Chemistry (MBDC) is the consulting service that grew out of the revolutionary "cradle to cradle" design theory. One of its first successes was a factory in Michigan where energy costs were reduced by 30 percent through an innovative solar heating and cooling system. MBDC claims that productivity at this concept-shattering factory, which cost only $15 million to build, has risen 24 percent, enabling the company to increase sales by $60 million a year with the same number of employees.[9]

MBDC was also a prime mover in the $2 billion renovation of Ford Motor's Dearborn, Michigan Rouge plant. The Rouge plant showcases a clean factory flooded with natural light. A grass roof and the reclamation of wetlands surrounding the plant keep storm water from emptying into the public system and reduce Ford's costs by some $35 million. Other companies using MBDC's ideas are Nike, marketing shoes that are virtually free of PVC and volatile organic chemicals; BASF, producing a new nylon that's infinitely recyclable; Steelcase Inc., which has produced a fabric for the seats of Lufthansa planes that is so free of toxins it can be eaten.[10]

A current priority for MBDC is the design of textiles that can be recycled or composted and that have no harmful chemicals. Working with Rohner Textil, a Swiss textile mill, they developed Climatex Lifecycle, a recyclable fabric for use in commercial upholstery and wall coverings. According to Albin Kalin, Rohner's CEO, trimmings from Climatex no longer need to be burned at a regulated incinerator and can be sold to gardening outlets for use as mulch or ground cover. Rohner's waste processing costs have been significantly reduced while MBDC's original concept has been commercially validated.[11]

Carrying out these important design changes might require some customers to start leasing products rather than buying them outright. The lease would be timed to expire at the end of the useful life of the product. The manufacturer would then collect and replace the old product, break down its complex materials into biological and technical nutrients that could be recycled into new products and resold to other customers.[12] Carpet manufacturers, such as BASF, have designed carpets to be easily dissolved or disassembled and have begun to sell these reconfigured "products" as "services." Ian Wolstenholme, BASF's carpeting sales and marketing manager describes the process as follows: "It's like an ice cube. We can freeze and unfreeze it as many times as we like."[13] The advantages of this process include saving a substantial amount of valuable raw materials as well as the elimination of useless or dangerous waste that is harmful to the environment. Manufacturing costs are reduced and a good part of the savings is passed on to the consumer.[14]

CEOs of many companies are becoming increasingly aware that deficiencies in today's design procedures lead to the use of potentially dangerous ingredients and a large amount of toxic waste. Everything from computers to sneakers contains chemicals that have yet to be tested for safety when they are used for their stated purpose or when recycled into the ground and water supply during the disposal process. Recognizing that there is no safe "away," the European Union has passed "end-of-life" legislation requiring automakers to recycle or reuse at least 80 percent of inoperative cars by 2006. Peter J. Pestillo, chairman of auto parts manufacturer Visteon Corporation, believes Europe's initiative will spread to the U.S. According to Pestillo, "Bill [McDonough] is getting us to believe that if we start early enough, we can avoid environmental problems altogether rather than correcting them little by little."[15]

The key is to create industrial processes that follow natural principles by replenishing, restoring and nourishing all other systems. Earth's primary nutrients—carbon, hydrogen, oxygen and nitrogen—are constantly recycled by natural processes. Humans, on the other hand, take substances from the earth and use them in ways that hamper their safe return to the soil. McDonough and Braungart believe that we can achieve sustainable prosperity only by imitating natural systems that effectively do away with waste. The materials in products, packaging and systems must determine the design, so that biological nutrients can return to the earth and technical materials can be recycled into the industrial process.[16]

Sharing *US*

> *One of the lessons of September 11 is that we are beginning to understand there is a combustible mix of poverty, lack of education, coupled with poor governance in states that are not necessarily failed, but are weak in many respects. It is in our enlightened self-interest to address those problems.*
>
> Nancy Birdsall,
> President, Center for Global Development[17]

It seems counterintuitive that one would work hard to earn money and then turn around and give it away. Economists find such selfless actions baffling and have been studying acts of altruism to uncover a more plausible self-interest rationale. One study found that people gave more willingly if their altruism was counterbalanced by some self-serving reciprocity. Accordingly, many charities now make an effort to reward their donors in an economical but meaningful manner. Whether motivated more by the guilt of having so much or the fulfillment that comes from helping the less fortunate, individual generosity is increasing rapidly, particularly by the affluent. But even those who have accumulated more modest wealth are searching for appropriate outlets to dispose of their largesse. Both groups seem to be following Andrew Carnegie's sage advice, "the man who dies rich dies disgraced."

One noteworthy philanthropist is Edward Scott Jr., co-founder of BEA Systems, a large software company. He became concerned about skyrocketing Third World debt with all its negative implications. After studying the issues and speaking with experts in the field, he decided to pledge $25 million to establish the Center for Global Development. His think tank is devoted to studying the impact of globalization on the poor. The Center uses a combination of policy-based research, strategic communications and targeted outreach to educate and engage both the public and government officials on global development issues. It claims to be the only organization of its kind dedicated to helping the poorest countries by advocating for well-researched policy changes in the richest ones.[18]

While Scott's pledge is undoubtedly one of the largest individual donations aimed at reducing global poverty and inequality, it is far from the only such donation. Globalization has had a significant impact on worldwide philanthropy for a number of reasons. First, the breadth and rapidity of global communications has heightened awareness of worldwide poverty and the agencies that serve the poor. There is also a growing realization that everyone's fate is inextricably tied to the well-being of all humanity. Second, the economic benefits of globalization have enabled a growing number of people to enjoy a higher standard of living; these beneficiaries are now able to donate some of their surplus wealth with little financial sacrifice. And third, there is an increasing recognition that, when sufficient resources are committed, our most troublesome problems—poverty and disease—can be successfully surmounted. For many of the affluent, the rising probability of success turns charitable giving into more of an obligation than an option.[19]

New organizations and services have been launched to facilitate this mounting interest in helping the global community. These enterprises highlight the plight of the disadvantaged and provide an outlet for those who desire to serve the general welfare. The pleasure that comes from generous and unreserved charity is enormous. It is wise to remember, "A vessel that is closed cannot be filled any more than it can be emptied."[20]

Many of these new donors are entrepreneurs who want to be personally involved in the causes they select and want to ensure their gifts are spent wisely. Some business pioneers have developed innovative structures that make it easier for people to become actively involved in the non-profit world. Doug Mellinger, a former software company CEO, is now CEO of Foundation Source which has developed the technology to enable wealthy individuals to set up their own foundations quickly and at a fraction of the usual cost. According to Mellinger, "we have a social revolution going on that will have an unbelievable impact on this country and the rest of the world."[21]

Community foundations and donor-advised funds are two rapidly growing conduits for charitable contributions. The latter has been referred to as the "poor man's private foundation" and is a growing force in philanthropy. These public charities have played a significant role in increasing charitable giving by making it easy, efficient and cost-effective. Donor-advised funds, for example, make it possible for someone with a modest amount of money—$10,000—to establish a personal foundation. The Vanguard Charitable Endowment Program is one of the largest of these donor-advised upstarts. It has partnered with United Way International, the independent overseas arm of the large U.S. charity, to meet the growing desire of its donors to help people throughout the world. As one of Vanguard's early global donors stated, "The world is becoming more interdependent. We have to think beyond our own shores."[22]

Contrary to expectations, philanthropy is surprisingly robust in some of the poorest nations of the world. For instance, the first-ever national survey of individual giving in Pakistan conducted in 1998 found that the average Pakistani gave 1.9 percent of his or her personal income per year. This compares with the 1999 per capita cash contribution in America of 1.8 percent. While there is no central source for analyzing data on global donations, indigenous philanthropy appears to be on the rise. Throughout Latin America, groups of institutions, foundations and enterprises donate cash and human resources to a variety of social welfare programs. The Hogar de Cristo Foundation, established in Chile in 1944, is a good example of a charitable organization thriving in a developing country. With 500,000 members and over 3,500 volunteers located in Chile's 11 regions, it receives millions of dollars in individual cash donations every year.[23]

The beneficiaries of world trade increasingly recognize their obligation to share the bounty. Capitalism, often derided as a cause of economic inequality, is fast becoming a tool for reducing poverty. The entrepreneurs and executives participating in this philanthropic upsurge are beginning to eclipse the relatively few EntrepreneurCelebs who became infamous for their selfish behavior. This generosity is evidence of enlightened self-interest—the belief that improving the lives of the needy all over the world will also improve our own.

Monetary contributions, while critically important, will not solve our global problems. James D. Wolfensohn, president of the World Bank group, made this point most eloquently when he said, "…whether they live on the plains or in the valleys, whether they live in slums or isolated villages, whether they speak Hindi, Swahili or Uzbek, they have one thing in common: They do not want charity. They want a chance. They do not want solutions imposed from without. They want the opportunity to build from within. They do not want my culture or yours. They want their own. They want a future enriched by the inheritance of their past."[24]

Engaging *US*

> *We... need a commitment to explicitly winning the battle of ideas... an inclusive notion of community where people are proud of their religions, their ethnic, their racial, their political convictions. But they're more than happy to be part of ever-larger communities of people... to nonviolent resolution with disputes, and this proposition that everybody counts, so we do better when we work together. Now, we have to explicitly **engage** this.*
> William Jefferson Clinton, Former President of the United States of America[25]

I first heard about Seeds of Peace at a presentation given by a former counselor who worked at the organization's summer camp. After the presentation, I viewed a film of a group of amiable, fun-loving teenagers who, prior to this experience, had nothing but enmity and distrust for one another. Watching the incredible breakthroughs brought tears of joy to my eyes.

Seeds of Peace was founded in 1993 by the late award-winning author and journalist John Wallach. The purpose of the organization is to foster peaceful coexistence around the world by bringing together teenagers from regions of conflict before fear, suspicion and prejudices permanently mold their view of the "enemy." As stated so eloquently on their web site, "Treaties are negotiated by governments. Peace is made by people." The program, aimed at nurturing lasting relationships, has grown from 46 participants in 1993 to around 2000 teenagers from the Middle East, Cyprus, Greece, Turkey, the Balkans, India, Pakistan, Afghanistan and the

United States. These future leaders, selected by their respective governments, come together for an intense month-long summer camp, where they learn that their common needs, desires and aspirations are much more important than their superficial differences. After they return home, graduates become part of a year-round program designed to build on the conflict resolution skills and close personal relationships developed at camp. Leaders throughout the world—Kofi Annan, George W. Bush, King Abdullah, Yasser Arafat, Yitzhak Rabin, Shimon Peres, Benjamin Netanyahu and Ehud Barak—have all given their strong support. The organization has received wide media attention and the UNESCO prize for Tolerance and Non-Violence.

Shortly after the September 11, 2001 attacks on America, Seeds of Peace convened the International Youth Summit on Uprooting Hatred and Terrorism at the United Nations in New York City. One hundred and twenty "Seeds" from twenty-two nations created a thirty-one page Charter to address the root causes of violent conflicts throughout the world. The Charter begins:

> *"Do not dismiss this as youthful idealism. Many of us live in places where killing and humiliation, poverty and homeless refugees are commonplace. We're surrounded by an atmosphere of hatred created by unjust realities. Violence does not begin when a gun is pointed or rock is thrown, but in the hate filled graffiti and political posters decorating the walls of our cities. When this takes physical expression in acts of terror, the victims often call for revenge, perpetuating the cycle of violence. Yet as Seeds of Peace, we have experienced real equity, unity, understanding and joy. Having faced a stark contrast, we now refuse to accept what is when we know what can be, if we truly implement these principles in our homes and our hearts. We refuse to be victims. We know it is possible to*

redirect human passions, even calls for revenge, toward the positive goal of creating peace."[26]

Excerpts from the Charter's principles call for an overhaul of the way many people are prejudicially educated and undemocratically governed. It goes on to state emphatically, "All people are responsible for each other." As such, there needs to be a global effort to diminish the economic disparities within society. "It is our duty, as well as privilege, as citizens of the world, to cooperate in order to bring prosperity to each other."[27] The young people engaged in Seeds of Peace programs can be instrumental in healing even the most hardened hatreds; a key step on the road to eliminating some of our most intractable global conflicts and turning sponsors of terror into promoters of peace.

Proclaiming *US*

Never doubt that a small group of thoughtful committed citizens can change the world; indeed it's the only thing that ever has.

Margaret Mead

The Earth Charter is a declaration of principles aimed at building a just, sustainable and peaceful global community. It asserts that environmental protection, human rights, equitable development and peace are interrelated and inseparable and challenges people everywhere to re-examine their values and choose the kind of world they want to create.

The drafting of the Earth Charter was begun at the 1992 Rio Earth Summit. In 1994 Mikhail Gorbachev, president of Green Cross International, and Maurice Strong, chairman of the Earth Council, began a new Earth Charter initiative with the support of the Dutch government. The product of a decade-long cross-cultural discussion, the drafting of the Earth Charter involved the most open, participatory consultation process ever for an international document. It has been written and refined by thousands of individuals worldwide, some experts in their fields, others from grassroots community organizations. The ideas and values in the Earth Charter are based on contemporary science, international law, the wisdom of spiritual and philosophical traditions around the world, United Nations' summit conferences, declarations and treaties made over past years and best practices. A benchmark draft was circulated internationally and the Commission approved the final version in Paris in March 2000.

The mission of the Earth Charter Initiative is to build a sustainable world based on respect for nature, human rights, economic justice and a desire for peace. The Secretariat for the Earth Charter, based in Costa Rica, coordinates activities for a global network of dozens of national committees and a wide variety of cooperating organizations. A website (*www.earthcharter.org*), maintained by the Secretariat, provides links to programs and organizations worldwide that disseminate, promote and encourage the implementation of the Charter by businesses, governments and citizen organizations at all levels.

The Charter's afterword states in part,

> *"Life often involves tensions between important **values** [emphasis added]. This can mean difficult choices. However, we must find ways to harmonize diversity with unity, the exercise of freedom with the common good, short-term objectives with long-term goals."*[28]

An important contribution of the Earth Charter is its higher-level soul values that enhance the quality of life for us all. A full description, including Preamble and Afterword can be found on the Earth Charter website.

Waking Up

There is a well-known parable about a boiled frog, the moral of which is relevant to this discussion. It can be paraphrased as follows: A frog placed in a pot of hot water will jump out in reaction to the life-threatening rise in temperature. Another frog put into a pot of lukewarm water will likely remain submerged in the pot even as the water temperature is gradually raised. Because of the slow increase in temperature, the frog will never sense the danger and will eventually succumb to the heat and be boiled to death. In the same way, slow but steady threats to our lives can mesmerize us—lull us to sleep—and prevent us from recognizing impending danger.[29] Previous chapters have detailed the perils of ill-conceived strategies that ignore environmental constraints, politically motivated policies that favor the few while harming the majority and business leaders that usurp disproportionate amounts of the output of the enterprise. Like the second frog, we have been immersed in the water while it approaches boiling; we have accepted indefensible policies and global turbulence as inevitable. We fail to react to global troubles or recognize the distortions that result from *ME*- and *THEM*-thinking. Other choices are available; we don't have to wait for our leaders to face challenges they would rather ignore. We can take a stand and choose a different path; a better set of values. The programs and organizations discussed above are just a few examples of those that should alert us to how hot the water is getting. They are leaders in envisioning and encouraging a just, prosperous and sustainable world, where all individuals realize their full potential while supporting their global neighbors in achieving theirs.

Notes

[1] Denise Breton and Christopher Largent, *The Soul of Economies: Spiritual Evolution Goes to the Marketplace* (Wilmington, DE: Idea House Publishing Company, 1991), 152.

[2] Richard Barrett, *Liberating the Corporate Soul: Building a Visionary Organization* (Boston: Butterworth-Heinemann, 1998), 41–42.

[3] Janine Benyus, *Biomimicry* (New York: Morrow, 1997), 1.

[4] William McDonough and Michael Braungart, *Cradle to Cradle: Remaking the Way We Make Things* (New York: North Point Press, a division of Farrar, Straus and Giroux, 2002), 128.

[5] Ibid., 41–43.

[6] Ibid., 27.

[7] Ibid., 59.

[8] Ibid., 86.

[9] Michelle Conlin and Paul Raeburn, "Industrial Evolution," *BusinessWeek,* 8 April 2002, 71.

[10] Ibid.

[11] Kerry A. Dolan, "Fabric Softener," *Forbes,* 15 April 2002, 112.

[12] Ibid., 111.

[13] Conlin, "Industrial Evolution," 72.

[14] McDonough, *Cradle to Cradle,* 114–115.

[15] Conlin, "Industrial Evolution," 71.

[16] McDonough, *Cradle to Cradle,* 131.

[17] Richard Morin and Claudia Deane, "Channel Surfing Brings Birth of Think Tank," *The Washington Post,* 27 November 2001, A11.

[18] Ibid.

[19] Susan Carey Dempsey, "Still Bullish on Boomers: an Interview with Paul Schervish," *Observations on Philanthropy, http://www.onphilanthropy.com*: 7 February 2003.

[20] *Pathwork Lecture 155* (Madison, VA: Pathwork Press), 7.

[21] Donna Fenn, "Shaking the Foundations," *Inc,* 1 May 2002.

[22] "A Breakthrough in Global Giving," *Giving Matters,* Fall 2001, 3–4.

[23] Susan Raymond, "Indigenous Philanthropy: Poorer Nations Also Give," *Observations on Philanthropy, http://www.onphilanthropy.com*:25 January 2002.

[24] James Wolfensohn, remarks in Hong Kong, 23 September 1997, *Around the World with United Way International, http://www.uwint.org/ aroundtheworld.html*: 8 February 2003.

[25] William Jefferson Clinton, transcript of a speech before the Council on Foreign Relations, "Our Shared Future: Globalization in the 21st Century," *Council on Foreign Relations, http://www.cfr.org/public/ Clinton_6-17-02_Transcript.html*: 17 June 2002.

[26] "Uprooting Hatred Violence and Terror," *The Olive Branch: Youth Magazine of the Seeds of Peace Program,* Winter 2002, 6.

[27] Ibid., 6–7.

[28] The Earth Charter: Values and Principles for a Sustainable Future, Organization Brochure (24 March 2000).

[29] John Renesch, "A Return to Freedom: Changing the Regime of Our Own Thinking," *Better Future News, http://www.renesch.com*: 17 December 2002.

Chapter Eleven

CompanyBuilding

The organizations discussed in the last chapter direct their efforts toward raising consciousness—making people aware of new ways of thinking and acting. They engage and educate by making their deeds their message. "That's great," you say. "The rest of us have to earn a living wage; we work for companies that need to make a profit." The following abbreviated IBM commercial emphasizes just this point; a high-minded business plan without financial and technical viability is fruitless.

A Brilliant Plan

CEO: *You've all read this.*
(The CEO reverently holds and reveals the "book," the work product of the consultants.)
Top shelf consultants.
Two million bucks.

> *Pure. Strategic. Thinking.*
> *Could put us years ahead…*
> *The board is psyched. I'm psyched.*
> *It's a brilliant plan.*

Pause

> *One question. Given our current technology, is this implementable?*

Pause

Woman 1:	No
Man 2:	No
Group:	No
Voiceover:	*Strategies you can actually execute,… Now there's a plan.*[1]

The strategic plan of any organization must be executable or it is worthless. Values-driven idealism must be combined with results-driven pragmatism. This chapter describes the best practices of four profit-seeking businesses that have applied both skill and resolve to build enterprises integrating sound financial practices with life-enriching soul values and, thereby, achieve sustainable prosperity. These companies espouse several of the soul values previously discussed: we have emphasized that value that sets each company apart.

Holistic Construction

> *Much of the innovation and prosperity that has occurred over the past century has been at great cost to the world we live in, especially to the environment… We have seen the shrinking of forests around the globe, the pollution of the atmosphere and the loss of many species. But today we understand much more and can design our industrial and manufacturing processes to prevent unsustainable damage to the world we live in. As we*

*move forward, it is important to reverse environmental
degradation and provide products and services to the
people who need them in a sustainable way.*
Richard Pratt, Chairman, Visy Industries[2]

Visy Industries is one of the largest privately owned paper
recycling and packaging companies in the world. Established
in Melbourne, Australia in 1948 and employing more than
8,000 people in Australia, New Zealand and the United
States, Visy's revenues exceed $3 billion a year. Their slogan
"harvesting the urban forest"[3] is clearly descriptive of a company which operates eight state-of-the-art paper and recycling machines that process more than 1.4 million tons of
waste paper and cardboard each year—the equivalent of cutting more than 18 million trees. Greenhouse gases are
reduced significantly as is the amount of waste paper going
into landfills.[4]

Visy has developed its business by making popular, high-
quality products from other people's trash. New York City,
long noted for its trash problems, has actually saved money
by selling scrap paper collected from residents to Visy's
Staten Island facility.[5] This cradle-to-cradle approach is the
very essence of holistic creation, the first of the soul values
described in the last chapter. Visy is one of the few companies in the world that places sustainable development at the
center of its operations while simultaneously providing products and services that help others maximize natural resources
and minimize damage to the environment.

When I toured Visy's mammoth Staten Island recycling
operation with plant management, I couldn't help but be
impressed by the scope and efficiency of the largest manufacturing facility built in New York City in more than 50
years. The site recycles 380,000 tons of post-consumer waste
paper annually and saves the equivalent of 13,500 trees per

day. New York City waste paper is transported to the site primarily by barge, reducing traffic congestion by more than 22,000 truck trips per year. Viewing the $200 million plant from a catwalk several stories above ground level, I watched countless forms of waste paper being offloaded from barges and dumped into a huge pit. A monstrous metal claw seizes a 7-ton handful of everything from computer printouts to pizza boxes and releases it into a huge blender that emulsifies the paper products as they hit the whirling blades. A series of machines continues the recycling process by squeezing, drying and pressing the contents until immense rolls of smooth, clean paper are produced at the opposite end of the mill.[6] Visy's plant is an exception to the rule: garbage in isn't always garbage out.

As is appropriate but rare, Visy takes a long-term view when it comes to promoting sustainability. They have an educational program for local school children aimed at developing a society-wide penchant for recycling. Using informative and entertaining videos plus animated coloring and comic books, Visy's resource kit for kindergarten through 5th grade makes learning about the three R's (reduce, reuse and recycle) an exciting experience. After explaining the benefits of recycling as well as the problems that arise when products are not recycled, a contest is held. The class that collects the most recyclable trash in a given period of time is rewarded with a pizza party. These students may not yet be the trash disposal decision makers at home but they can be influential in the short term and make a real difference when they start their own households. Visy, the environment and society at large all benefit from this far-sighted program.[7]

Visy has won many awards over the last several years: the prestigious Triple Bottom Line Award from the Australian Institute of Engineers, The Victorian Premier's Business Sustainability Awards for achieving U. S. Food and Drug

Administration (FDA) approval for its curbside plastics recycling initiative and the United Nations Association of Australia Award for its environmental best practices programs. Commenting on the United Nations award Visy's CEO, Harry Debney said:

> *Visy had built its business in the belief that it is possible and highly desirable for excellent environmental and business performance to go hand in hand... Visy's commitment to environmental best practices is integral to the business' day-to-day functions—it's something we're passionate about and which forms an important part of our decision making on everyday issues and all major projects.*[8]

Visy's commitment to sustainable development ensures its activities and products enhance the environment. To this end, Visy develops innovative processes that recover waste and transform it into valuable recycled products, adds primary materials only when they enhance the viability of waste recycling and works with suppliers, customers, governments and the community to reduce waste production. These benefits substantiate the statement of Tufts University economist and recycling expert, Frank Ackerman, that recycling prevents almost incalculable costs from being levied on society.[9] The company aims for continuous improvement through rigorous training, compliance oversight, community consultation and extensive research and development.[10]

Visy reinvests more than $20 million per year in research and development to maintain its best practices and keep a competitive edge on its products and services. As an example, a recent $10 million investment in innovative glass processing technology is expected to reduce the amount of glass being sent to landfills by up to 30,000 tons per year. In addition, more than 95 percent of Visy Board's boxes are produced from 100 percent recycled paper. Fifty thousand tons of new Kraft paper are still needed each year to maintain product strength as fiber breaks down from repeated use. To meet this need, Visy designed a cutting-edge Kraft pulp mill at Tumut in the Australian Alps. The mill introduces new technologies and processes and is designed to the highest environmental standards. The mill consumes relatively little water and a significant proportion of the energy used in the mill is "green," generated on site using atmosphere-friendly biomass fuels such as bark and wood waste. The environmental aspects of the project were complemented by a socially responsible construction approach emphasizing extensive community consultation throughout the planning, approval and implementation phases.[11]

Visy began, as have many successful companies, by recognizing a need and then creating products to meet that need; at the same time providing financial rewards for its investors. Numerous environmental and social benefits have resulted from their activities. In addition to the extensive environmental contributions detailed above, Visy donates around $10 million each year (more than 3 percent of world wide pretax profit) to various causes. Richard Pratt, Visy Chairman, says, "It's amazing, the more money we give away, the more money the company makes. Generosity works." This quote is a perfect segue into our next model company and the soul value of sharing generously.

Giving and Receiving—A Continuum

When I realized that it would be necessary to travel overseas to conduct personal interviews and field research for this book, South Africa with its rich but disquieting history, seemed a superb place to start. Joan and I concluded we couldn't go to South Africa and not visit a safari game reserve.

We had been on safari (the photographic kind) in Kenya more than a decade before and had enjoyed a magically inspiring time—we couldn't forgo the opportunity for another visit. Choosing among all the possible lodges in and around the famous Kruger National Park was initially quite difficult. Eventually we happened on an Internet description of Djuma Game Reserve and were struck by its location, facilities and enlightened philosophy. Situated in the renowned Sabi Sand Reserve that borders Kruger, Djuma (roar of the lion) comprises two properties with a total of 7000 hectares of traversing rights. The Game Reserve has 65 permanent staff and connects with a worldwide audience through its partial ownership of and active involvement in *Africam.com*. This extremely popular Internet web site, with more than 20 million hits per month, was the first virtual game reserve with live cameras providing real time, live footage from the wild and unpredictable bush in and around Djuma. During many of our game drives, we were accompanied by a cameraman who showed everything we saw to the rest of the world.

In the late 1980s, Jurie Moolman inherited the property that is now Djuma from his father. With a loan of 20,000 rand, he began to commercialize it in 1993. From the start, Jurie, a Ph.D. biologist, and his wife Pippa, with a fine arts background, were motivated by the desire to conserve the land for future generations. Moolman believes responsible commercialization should accentuate the African Savanna's natural wonders while respecting the culture and traditions of the surrounding community. To the extent the game reserve thrives, jobs in the neighboring communities are created. This gives the local residents a stake in the land and an incentive to protect and conserve the environment. Moolman believes by bringing formerly advantaged and disadvantaged sections of society together Apartheid wounds can be healed and a more prosperous and fulfilling future created.[12]

We have already seen that one of the legacies of South Africa's past is the wealth gap between blacks and whites. To close this chasm, skill levels in black communities must be upgraded. Jurie Moolman and his partners came up with an innovative solution to this problem as they built and expanded the game lodge. He spent several hours with us at breakfast one morning describing his approach to creating a new, more egalitarian South Africa.[13] During the building of the lodges on the Djuma reserve, heavy machinery was shunned in favor of local labor. Because the residents lacked certain construction skills, it was necessary to hire a white contractor from outside the area. As part of his agreement with the general contractor, Moolman insisted that black labor from the communities of Dixie and Utha (originally built as government reservations for local tribes) would be employed and the contractor agreed to train those local workers in building skills. Eventually, members of the community were able to develop a full-service construction company that is now doing work in Djuma's camps, as well as many other game lodges in the surrounding Sabi Sand Reserve. Insisting on these job-training activities meant increased project costs; yet Moolman considers the resulting benefits well worth the incremental expense. He told us that he is merely following his belief that, to create the new South Africa, everyone must work together as a single community.

Djuma has made it a priority to respect and share with the culture of the neighboring Shangaan tribe. Apartheid policies, and the resulting racial alienation, led to a lack of understanding and respect for the customs of the many African tribes. Moolman's empathy is evidenced by his statement, "When we forget this diversity we become arrogant and intolerant and prone to thinking 'our' way is the only way."[14] In 1999, when Vuyatela became Djuma's newest camp, Moolman decided that it would be important to respect the customs of those who work at the reserve. Local tribes were brought in to bless the new construction sites so ancestors could be informed of their intentions. The Sangoma, a traditional healer, "threw the bones"—the lie of the "bones" indicated that the ancestors were pleased! And in what may be a world first, these ancient rituals were broadcast live over the Internet on *Africam.com*.[15]

Djuma contributes to the local community in many other ways. Recycled, but still valuable, trash generated by the lodges is offered to the surrounding villages. Organic matter from the kitchens is used for pig fodder; brightly colored plastic packaging material found on many products is woven into tablemats and carpets by the local staff and either used by them or sold to visitors. Glass and metal waste gets sorted and sold to a nearby recycling company. The money earned from these efforts is used to pay for employee social events. Nearby Shangaan villagers have been employed to hand paint the chalets with a contest held for the best designs.[16]

With job creation crucial to South Africa's social and economic future, the Moolmans were delighted when they were presented with a business proposal that benefited both the local village and Djuma's guests. The idea was to incorporate cultural activities into the village trips already offered. Tourists are now taken to see the rituals of a Shangaan wedding ceremony and are entertained with traditional dancing and a sampling of local foods. Some 35 new jobs have been created as a result of the expanded village tour; a small example of how important the hospitality industry is in South Africa's economic growth plans.[17] When we went on the tour our personal safari tracker accompanied us and took us to see his house and meet a few of his many relatives. We were told how his employment at the game reserve enables him to provide for the needs of a large extended family. On our visit to Dixie Village, we visited the local crèche (pre-school) and primary school. Building and upgrading the educational facilities in the two adjacent communities, Dixie and Utha, is another place where Djuma's money and personnel are actively involved.

Children from these villages need to compete in the global economy yet the kids come from households without books and families that have never been to a library. The Moolmans began their quest to improve educational opportunities of the surrounding communities by paying for the completion of a half-finished crèche in Utha. This resulted in the creation of several jobs and the appreciation of 80 young children. Since the crèche was able to raise only about half of its ongoing financial requirements, a good part of which is Djuma's monthly contribution, the Moolmans began to solicit money from corporations doing business in South Africa. Working with others, they were able to convince seven companies to donate 1.6 million rand to the effort. A trust, administered by Djuma, has funded such necessities as desks and chairs plus the renovation and construction of classrooms for a primary and high school in Utha and a primary school and crèche in Dixie.[18] In addition, Moolman and his partner were able to convince Nelson Mandela to visit and officially open the Utha crèche. While everyone involved was enthralled by Mandela's towering presence, the children will be the real beneficiaries long after the event is forgotten.[19] Realizing that an educated citizenry is vital to the progress of South Africa, Djuma continues its community involvement whenever and however it can.

Many companies give back to the communities in which they operate. I am unaware, however, of any company more dedicated to building its business in a way that complements and enhances the cultural traditions of the community as well as its educational and job creation opportunities.

The Power of Effective Engagement

Organization leaders who desire to make a difference in the world—improve the planet in some tangible way—cannot do so by complaining about the current state of affairs. They must be willing to engage some part of the population and actively participate in transforming it. In the world of big business, it is hard to find a best practices engagement model more successful and rewarding than United Parcel Service's (UPS) Community Internship Program (CIP). Begun in 1968, the program actively involves company managers in several hands-on community service projects. Jim Casey, UPS' founder, believed that the only way to understand someone else is to walk in their shoes. Participants are taken off the job (at full pay) for one month and immersed in existing community projects where they are exposed to people from a variety of disadvantaged backgrounds and circumstances. Fifty managers are chosen annually and placed in one of several sites: the Henry Street Settlement—a social services agency on the Lower East Side of New York City, a parochial school in Chicago, the Mexican-American Cultural Center in McAllen, Texas and the University of Tennessee at Chattanooga where interns work with southern Appalachian poor. The settings are very different but the problems of modern industrial society—poverty, homelessness, spousal abuse, drugs, crime and gang warfare—are common to them all.[20]

During their month of service, interns live in the community in accommodations that can only be described as austere. They interact with a wide variety of people ranging from illegal immigrants to impoverished street people. They may go to prisons, ride in police cars, meet with social service organizations, talk to AIDS patients, help drug addicts or aid the homeless. They are required to keep daily logs of their activities and have the opportunity to discuss their experiences with other interns and assigned social workers.[21] In one case, interns discovered that a local clinic was spending a majority of its budget to purify contaminated drinking water. The interns developed new methods to purify the water, thereby saving the clinic significant sums of money that are now used to provide medical care for the poor.[22]

This program is a great example of a win-win-win-win outcome. The community organizations benefit from high quality volunteers assisting them in their work. The people served by these programs see a large corporation that cares about more than just the bottom line. UPS benefits by developing managers with enhanced problem-solving skills and greater sensitivity in their interaction with people. The greatest effect seems to be on the interns themselves—giving them the opportunity to observe common longings and desires rather than dwelling on differences. Many managers report they come away with a more compassionate view of their compatriots and a greater appreciation for the blessings they have personally received. They realize one person can make a difference and they often become more involved in their own communities. Several comments from graduates give a clear indication of the impact of the program. "I thought I would be the one giving to the local community. Instead, I was the one who received so much more." "The internship program has opened my eyes to look for the potential in people rather than their faults. I feel I have become more effective at making situations work rather than giving up. I'll do what I can to teach, mentor, volunteer, and become an asset to my community." "I feel so much good has come from just a little kindness. We've made a major impact in a few lives—including my own."[23]

More than 1,200 UPS managers have been through the program which costs the company about $10,000 dollars per intern or approximately $500,000 annually. This is a significant commitment for a publicly owned, profit-making enterprise. The benefits to UPS from the program, although difficult to quantify, are, nonetheless, meaningful. After managers return to work their interactions with employees are much less rigid and far more empathetic. As a result, grievances are reduced and the employee turnover rate is unusually low. Most managers are eager to participate in an internship as part of their career development plan. Perhaps the best indication of the value UPS places on the program is the fact that they have never curtailed funding even when the budget was tight and other projects were reduced or eliminated.

As one intern observed, "After my CIP experience, I am better prepared to handle situations at work. Long training seminars and discussions about diversity are beneficial, but the best way to positively impact managers is to provide opportunities for first hand experiences."[24] These comments reflect a level of engagement that few corporate programs have matched. To quote the best selling book, *The Power of Full Engagement,* "To be fully engaged, we must be physically energized, emotionally connected, mentally focused and spiritually aligned with a purpose beyond our immediate self-interest."[25] The CIP serves the common good as it touches the intern, the company and the community on each of these four levels.

Putting It All Together

The White Dog Café is a culinary landmark in the Philadelphia region and widely recognized throughout the nation (named by Conde Nast as one of the 50 best restaurants in the country) and indeed in many parts of the world. Quite an accomplishment for a business that has a relatively modest $5 million in annual revenues and employs a staff of around 100 people.[26] In addition to providing excellent food and attentive service, the White Dog Café, along with The Black Cat Gift Shop in the adjoining building, strives to be a place where people can connect with one another and enhance their understanding of world issues.

Creating Holistically

Judy Wicks, the founder and owner of the White Dog and Black Cat, continually strives to think and act holistically by considering how her decisions impact employees, customers, the community and natural environment. Employees are paid above industry salaries and given some unusual perks including the opportunity to travel overseas on White Dog sponsored trips at a considerable discount. At a time of inflated executive pay, a 5:1 ratio is maintained between the highest- and lowest-paid White Dog employees, Wicks included.[27] In an industry where salaries and employee satisfaction are notoriously low, White Dog employees feel valued and appreciate being kept informed about important community and world issues. As a result, turnover is much lower than industry norms.

The menu changes with the season to take advantage of fresh organic produce and humanely raised meats purchased, whenever possible, from local family farms. Obviously, the customers benefit from enjoying fresh and healthy food. In addition, Wicks believes small family farms are true protectors of the soil—they are holistically sensitive, they generate less waste, are concerned about the environment and are more attentive to worker satisfaction and quality of life issues.

Sharing Generously

The White Dog serves the community far beyond its employees, customers and suppliers. Twenty percent of its profits are contributed to fund the wide-ranging programs of its charitable foundation. In addition, Wicks takes the unusual posture of establishing cooperative relationships with would-be competitors and partners with minority-owned restaurants to encourage customers to visit neighborhoods they might otherwise not frequent. Developing a mentoring program for students, an inner city gardening tour and a "Fair Food Project" to help build the supply lines between sustainable farmers and urban markets are a few of the ways she shares her talents and enthusiasm.

Wicks is a strong advocate, both philosophically and financially, for The Reinvestment Fund (TRF), a community development financial institution dedicated to building wealth and opportunity for low-income communities and low-and moderate-income individuals. Investors in TRF generally accept below market rates of return with the understanding that their money is invested in projects that support the poor and disadvantaged in the community. Since 1985 TRF's financing has created over 7,500 affordable housing units, added 3 million square feet of community facilities and 5,600 child care slots and preserved more than 100 small businesses while adding in excess of 12,000 jobs.[28] When Judy Wicks believes in something she is willing to back it wholeheartedly; she wrote a very persuasive letter to potential investors encouraging them to invest in TRF. The extent of her influence is reflected in the fact that the letter attracted more new investors than any of the Fund's previous promotional efforts.

Engaging Tolerantly

Wicks gets great satisfaction from publicizing the joys of civic engagement to her customers. "I use good food to lure innocent customers into social activism."[29] The White Dog offers a multitude of diverse community programs designed to increase awareness, build community and contribute to a more just and peaceful world. Local tours and community service days are also popular with the White Dog's patrons. According to sociologist Ray Oldenburg, "Every great civilization has such places... they are the heart of the community's social vitality, the grassroots of the democracy; without them, the diversity of human contact diminishes and citizens become estranged."[30]

Bringing people together is one thing, doing it profitably is quite another. Wicks meets this challenge by following her often overlooked but impressive pragmatic instincts. Slow business nights have been enlivened and made more profitable by popular lectures and ad-lib storytelling by prominent individuals and everyday customers. Wicks began her restaurant career as a waitress in a neighborhood restaurant and used her entrepreneurial skills to bring the White Dog Café to its current level of success. As a result, she believes strongly in the power of the free market. She told me that the business has been a driving force in her life as it has given her the freedom and opportunity to be at her creative best.[31]

Wicks works tirelessly both locally and internationally promoting and supporting issues that are often ignored or unconventional. At home, she has long been a leader in the socially responsible business movement and a frequent speaker at such functions. The White Dog sponsors trips to visit ten "sister" restaurants all over the world including Nicaragua, Vietnam, Cuba, Mexico and Lithuania. One of the goals for the international restaurant program is to demonstrate how free enterprise can be a force which benefits ordinary citizens: "In countries that have been burnt by capitalism, where companies have mistreated workers or the environment, we try to show that it's not always like that. Capitalism *can* serve the common good."[32] When traveling she buys products from low-income artisans that frequently have a socially responsible cause connected to them. Many of these items turn up in the Black Cat Gift Shop; Wicks considers the unusual bric-a-brac and offbeat gifts that she gathers from around the world a way to raise the social consciousness of her customers while providing financial support to worthy small enterprises.

Proclaiming Humbly

An individual who creates holistically, shares generously, and engages tolerantly has established the credibility to help others see the benefits of integrating soul values into every facet of a business. Based on her many accomplishments, accolades and awards, and the fact that she lives her principles fully, Judy Wicks of the White Dog Café, has achieved this select status.

The last two chapters have shown how profit and non-profit organizations alike have successfully incorporated *US*-dominant soul values into their operations. The final chapter discusses how communities around the world have begun devising innovative approaches, aligned with soul values, to address a variety of problems.

Notes

[1] *A Brilliant Plan*, script of a television commercial (Ogilvy & Mather, 2001).

[2] "Overview," *Visy Industries, http://www.visy.com.au/overview*: 2003.

[3] Gretel H. Schueller, "Wasting Away: Is Recycling on the Skids?" *Onearth*, Fall 2002, 21.

[4] "Overview."

[5] Schueller, "Wasting Away," 22.

[6] Ibid., 21.

[7] Daryl Whitehead, interview by author (Staten Island, NY: 25 May 2003).

[8] "Visy Wins United Nations Award for Environmental and Business Performance," *Visy News, http://www.visy.com.au/news/news_detail.asp?id=23*: 24 February 2003.

[9] Schueller, "Wasting Away," 22.

[10] "Overview."

[11] Ibid.

[12] Jurie Moolman, "History and Philosophy," *Djuma Game Reserve, http://www.djuma.com/history.htm*: 4 May 2003.
[13] Jurie Moolman, interview by author, tape recording (Hluvukani, South Africa: 9 November 2002).
[14] Jurie Moolman, "Vuyatela Sangoma," *Djuma Game Reserve, http://www.djuma.cum/Vuyatela_sangoma.htm*: 17 April 1999.
[15] Moolman, "Vuyatela Sangoma".
[16] Pippa Moolman, "Let's Talk Trash," *Drum Beat—News from Djuma Game Reserve, http://www.djuma.com/drumbeat0702.htm*: July 2002.
[17] Pippa Moolman, "New Structure to Our Cultural Village Trips," *Drum Beat—News from Djuma Game Reserve, http://www.djuma.com/drumbeat0402.htm*: April 2002.
[18] Jurie Moolman, "Nwa-Tumberi Crèche," *Djuma Game Reserve, http://www.djuma.com/creche.htm*: September 1999.
[19] Jurie Moolman, "Madiba Magic," *Djuma Game Reserve, http://www.djuma.com/mandela.htm*: June 2001.
[20] Cal Darden, "Delivery on Diversity Leadership: a Walk in the Other Guy's Shoes," *UPS, http://www.ups.com/content/us/en/about/executive/speech/dard...*: 28 April 2003.
[21] Ibid.
[22] Bob Filipczak, "25 Years of Diversity at UPS," *Training: The Human Side of Business*, August 1992.
[23] "Community Internship Program," *UPS—Community Causes, http://www.community.ups.com/community/causes/us_relations/*: 28 April 2003.
[24] Steve Sinclair, "Diary of a Community Internship," *UPS—Community Scrapbook, http://www.community.ups.com/community/scrapbook/employee*: 28 April 2003.
[25] Jim Loehr and Tony Schwartz, *The Power of Full Engagement* (New York: Free Press, a division of Simon & Schuster, Inc., 2003).
[26] "White Dog Café: Living Economy Award," *Business Ethics*, Fall 2002, 11.
[27] Ibid.
[28] *The Reinvestment Fund 2001 Annual Report* (Philadelphia, PA: 2002).
[29] David Bollier, *Aiming Higher: 25 Stories of How Companies Prosper by Combining Sound Management and Social Vision* (New York: AMACOM, a division of American Management Association, 1996), 250.
[30] Ibid., 245.
[31] Judy Wicks, interview by author, tape recording (Philadelphia, PA: 21 April 2003).
[32] Bollier, *Aiming Higher*, 249.

Chapter Twelve

CommunityCreating

The de facto economic model of a country usually evolves with relatively little planning or forethought; once ensconced it is rarely challenged. Exceptions occur during times of social upheaval and political or economic discontent. Argentina and Brazil offer two good examples; their economic problems engendered radical changes throughout most areas of life. The first part of this chapter will touch upon a number of the innovative changes taking place in both of these countries and the applicability of these innovations to the rest of the world.

A more profound shift has taken place recently in the United States where corporate scandals and executive malfeasance have outraged many formerly content capitalists. This rising dissatisfaction has encouraged a group of social entrepreneurs to form an alliance of local businesses with common values and community interests. The potential significance of this movement to the globalization process will be discussed in greater detail in the second part of the chapter.

Reviving Argentina

Argentina's economic collapse led to significant disruptions in the flow of the most basic products and forced many citizens into alternative methods of exchanging vital goods and services. As a result of this upheaval, neighborhood groups organized corner soup kitchens, staples replaced money as admission to cultural events and neighbors grew food in community gardens. Most notable, however, was the upsurge in worker cooperatives, the proliferation in neighborhood assemblies and the explosion of worker barter clubs.

Worker cooperatives are not a new concept in Argentina, but their numbers rose dramatically as bankrupt companies were taken over by workers in an effort to assure their continued ability to earn a living. For instance, the 147 employees of IMPA, a bankrupt manufacturer of aluminum containers, responded to their predicament with ingenuity and solidarity. By increasing productivity and converting to the use of less expensive scrap, raw material costs were reduced 40 percent. The company pays wages well above the national average; everyone, including managers, receives the same amount.[1] Other cooperatives share a similar model; the workers elect "directors" to run the companies and profits are split among the "associates." While not everyone earns the same amount, the highest paid associate makes no more than a few times the lowest. The most immediate benefit of this movement has been the economic survival of many of Argentina's workers. A secondary effect is providing workers with a measure of control over their lives and a sense of shared goals within their communities.

The number and scope of barter clubs in Argentina increased significantly and is estimated to account for hundreds of millions of dollars worth of business. These barter clubs—exchange networks that use slips of paper called credits—attracted interest from a significant portion of the population and tempered the previously distinct social divisions.

Although subject to some abuses such as counterfeiting, they demonstrate how necessity can lead to innovative, unifying solutions. Psychologist Nilda Canon sees it as a welcome mechanism for psychological health. "It gets people out of their houses and interacting with one another."[2] Heloisa Primavera, a social economist, believes the barter economy fosters community over the isolationism that is often present in the traditional consumer-oriented society. "It's also a tool for replacing scarcity thinking with abundance thinking."[3]

Largely out of necessity, Argentines have learned to be more creative, tolerant, generous and engaging. In so doing they are exhibiting, to varying degrees, higher-level soul values. Making these soul values an integral part of the workplace as well as the larger community may explain, at least in part, why Argentina's economy has been more resilient than many pessimists expected.[4]

Rejuvenating Brazil

To a lesser degree, Brazil faces some of the same fiscal problems that haunt Argentina. President Luiz Inacio Lula da Silva's support comes mostly from Brazil's most disadvantaged citizens. Nonetheless he could not avoid instituting a number of traditional and perhaps unpalatable remedies such as raising interest rates and reducing spending to stabilize the rampant inflation and bloated debt. It took about a year and a half before the policies of the Lula administration began to revive Brazil's sagging economy. While great challenges remain, particularly in the areas of education and income inequality, the center-left that elected the former metal worker turned politician is guardedly optimistic about Brazil's future direction.

More significant, however, was President Lula's bold plan to help Brazil's poor become viable capitalists. A product of the slums himself, he has made closing the gap between the extravagantly prosperous and desperately poor a high priority. Wealthy Brazilians can secure capital by mortgaging their homes but the poor usually have no legal proof of ownership and are largely left out of the credit system. Lula wants to change this and enable Brazil's poor to gain formal title to their homes and, thereby, access to relatively inexpensive capital.[5]

According to Peruvian economist Hernando De Soto, "Developing countries… have [legal] systems designed for a few that now have to serve the many."[6] In his book, *The Mystery of Capital: Why Capitalism Triumphs in the West and Fails Everywhere Else,*" de Soto points out that, in many developing countries, the poor not only lack legal title to their homes, which could act as collateral for badly needed loans, but face virtually insurmountable regulatory obstacles. He articulately proposes a solution—streamline the titling of properties so that the value of the assets of the working poor (their homes) can be used to access funds needed for education or to start and build a business. I saw this problem quite clearly on a recent visit to Cuba. The Castro government has given homes (some quite luxurious) to most of its citizens but, lacking legal ownership, they are not permitted to sell them or use them for collateral. As a way of recognizing the store of value that these homes represent, a barter system has grown up and people trade homes among themselves.

There is no lack of entrepreneurial spirit in many developing countries; in Brazil and in Cuba, among others, poor people are continually starting businesses. The problem is that, with few exceptions, these businesses are outside the formal economy and, therefore, outside the protection of the law. The very foundations of capitalism—property rights, contracts, credit and capital—are absent; businesses unavoidably remain small and inefficient. Without adequate capital, these developing countries lose the creative energy of a large segment of the population and the potential tax revenue that would be available if these businesses did not operate in the underground economy. De Soto's ideas are not by themselves the solution; they must be supplemented by an improved educational system, the elimination of corruption and the reform of many cultural institutions. Nonetheless, De Soto's message has resonated with a wide segment of the political spectrum—from former Clinton administration Secretary of State Madeleine Albright to Reagan-era Housing and Urban Development Secretary Jack Kemp.[7]

Brazil has much work to do to stabilize its shaky financial situation. Sharing the fruits of the global economy with all its citizens, a key soul value, is a necessary prerequisite for building a strong sense of community and an enduring prosperity.

Rethinking Tradition

In the late 1980s, some U.S. business leaders established organizations to develop and promote socially responsible business (SRB) practices. Many local groups are affiliated with one or both of the national sustainable business organizations, Social Venture Network (SVN) and Business for Social Responsibility (BSR). SVN, founded in 1987, is an organization of several hundred business owners and leaders, private investors, social entrepreneurs, foundation officers and other cutting-edge thinkers. They share a commitment to building a just, sustainable and prosperous business environment through a variety of initiatives, information services and forums that strengthen and empower their members to work on behalf of their common vision. By design, the organization is limited in scope and function and does not seek to coordinate sustainable business networks at the community level.

BSR, on the other hand, is a global organization composed primarily of substantial national businesses and MNCs seeking to expand their commercial success while operating in an ethical manner that respects people, communities and the environment. Representing a wide range of industries and geographies, BSR companies account for over $2 trillion in annual sales. In 2001, BSR reorganized its operations and dropped support for local business networks that were addressing the needs of small and medium-sized businesses. This shift in BSR's emphasis together with the desire of many in the SRB movement to build an alternative to big, transnational businesses provided the impetus for the creation of a new organization. The new movement set out to address the deeper needs of employees and the surrounding community. Emphasis was placed on enhancing creativity and consciousness, building meaningful relationships and providing more fulfilling jobs. Leaders of this new organization gathered socially responsible business networks from across the U.S. and around the world that were committed to developing strong "local living economies" (LLEs). "Strengthening local economies shortens the separation between cause and effect, allowing business owners and customers to comprehend the environmental and social impacts of their behavior more immediately. It also results in economic interests meshing more effectively with community interests as it becomes clear how closely they overlap."[8]

An LLE is an economy built on life-enriching principles: the nurture of natural and community life coupled with long-term economic and environmental sustainability. Vibrant local economies work in concert with natural systems, support biological and cultural diversity and encourage fulfilling and enjoyable community life. In general, the operation of LLEs provides a sharp contrast to multinational corporations that dominate many aspects of society and influence much of the global economy. These enterprises are characterized by minimal involvement in the local community and by absentee owners who often have no knowledge of, and assume no liability for, the social and environmental consequences of actions taken on their behalf.

As an example, real estate developers from outside a community, as well as many national and international retailers, destroy woodlands to build shopping centers and housing complexes, with little concern about deleterious effects on the surrounding community. Urban sprawl, and the corresponding proliferation of asphalt-covered parking lots, reduces the ability of the remaining tree canopy to retain storm runoff and soak up vast quantities of pollutants and greenhouse gases. Municipalities are then forced to spend substantial sums for largely avoidable flood control systems and air quality improvements.[9] The non-profit organization, American Forests, in partnership with several U.S. governmental agencies, has conducted studies in some 20 metropolitan areas around the United States documenting the loss of tree cover of each region and the resulting harmful environmental and economic impact this causes.[10]

Because national developers may not experience the detrimental consequences of their actions they are less inclined to encourage full-cost pricing of energy, material and land or reduce waste and pollution. The quality of life in many communities deteriorates until local citizens become better informed and actively concerned about these issues. In LLEs, this is carried to its logical conclusion where those who suffer the consequences are the ones who make the decisions.[11]

BALLE Who

Local business networks in over a dozen North American cities and regions have now joined together to form a national network, Business Alliance for Local Living Economies (BALLE). BALLE expects the number of members to grow substantially in the next few years and envisions hundreds of affiliates within the foreseeable future. Internationally, groups in Vancouver and Toronto are looking to become the first non-U.S.-based communities to join BALLE; Mexican affiliates and communities not contiguous to the U.S. may not be far behind. The main criterion for joining the network is that members be dedicated to building socially, environmentally and financially sustainable economies by creating, supporting and connecting with other similarly oriented community businesses throughout the world.

As an alliance that facilitates local and regional organizations, BALLE does not determine local member policies. Member organizations, therefore, are autonomous and self-governed. "By bringing together networks of business owners and investors with leaders of other organizations dedicated to working locally for the common good, BALLE plans to forge new models that benefit communities—while boosting the bottom line of member businesses."[12]

Sustainable Business Network

The Sustainable Business Network (SBN), a non-profit organization in the Greater Philadelphia area, is one of BALLE's founding members. It is comprised of a variety of local business and community leaders who are committed to creating a more socially, environmentally and financially sustainable local economy. I first became familiar with SBN early in 2002 and have attended a number of their meetings. I have found that, although SBN's membership is diverse, they share all or most of the following values:

- Local ownership of businesses
- Protection and restoration of the natural environment
- An inclusive, diverse and vibrant community
- Maintaining a strong local culture and neighborhood character
- Support for independent media and bookstores

- Organic, humane and local agriculture
- Renewable energy and energy conservation
- Public transportation, bicycling and sustainably fueled vehicles
- Recycling, reusing and composting
- Mentoring, supporting and engaging community youngsters
- Community investment—savings reinvested in the community

Most of the values described above are in close alignment with the soul values described in Chapter 10. The Sustainable Business Network believes strongly in a holistic, sustainable view of life and encourages businesses to develop their products and services accordingly. Andrew Anderson, Director of the Greater Philadelphia Local Living Economy Fund, summarized SBN's goals: "We want to invest in goods and services, rather than bads and disservices."[13]

Insistence on diversity and inclusion corresponds to an *either/and* tolerance. Reinvesting in the community where one lives and works, even if returns are higher elsewhere, is a way to give back and share with the people and institutions that provide support. And engaging and educating the citizens of a community, from youngsters to seniors, about the virtues of LLEs is an example of fearlessly proclaiming views that are not currently favored by the mainstream and may be ridiculed by some as naive, impractical and/or too utopian. The validity of such critiques will be examined at the end of the chapter.

Serving the Community

SBN has established "building blocks" for a strong local economy. These are the products and services necessary to make a local economy sustainable and include: food, energy, clothing, healthcare and healing, cleaning and maintenance, housing (green building), transportation (alternative fuels), community capital and socially responsible investors, waste and recycling facilities, independent media, neighborhood arts and culture and a variety of craftspeople.

Entrepreneurs and leaders have begun to organize around their areas of interest and recruit like-minded members. Since local organizations may already be working in these areas, SBN invites them to join together to achieve greater efficiency and coordination. Creating educational programs, hosting regional conferences and designing local branding all aimed at strengthening the organization and developing strategic alliances.[14]

Consumer-to-business and business-to-business transactions are facilitated by the Web site constructed and initially funded by BALLE (*www.livingeconomies.org*). A database compiles products and services in various areas to promote local sourcing to all members. BALLE plans to expand this database internationally to support community-friendly businesses around the world. This is both a laudable and crucial goal; local economies, no matter how self-sufficient, cannot function in isolation. Polluted air and water cannot be confined to a particular region; unsustainable environmental practices anywhere in the world inevitably result in degrading the environment everywhere. One result is that those who implement responsible and, at least in the short term, more costly procedures, are at a disadvantage relative to those who are not as concerned about the environment. Obviously, any new idea must be tested and refined before it is widely expanded. The sooner BALLE can begin an international expansion the more meaningful will be its contribution.

SBN holds bimonthly meetings that provide an opportunity for networking with individuals who share similar interests and values. A second objective is to inform and educate members and the surrounding community about subjects and activities of common interest. Presentations offered at SBN's meetings have included: sources of community capital, recycling opportunities and challenges, alternative energy providers, low energy consumption transportation, and green "housekeeping" chemicals and materials. The meetings enable members to learn about products and services businesses in the community are providing. A meeting devoted to recycling featured a regional director of Verizon Communications, an environmental consultant and the president of a recycling company.

Verizon's presentation was particularly useful as everyone living or working in the Philadelphia area is affected by the policies of this multibillion-dollar global telecommunications company. Their recycling effort is quite extensive—they collect and recycle a wide variety of paper products, cans, bottles, batteries, tires, waste oil and laser printer cartridges. They also assist with local phone directory recycling programs. Those present were afforded the opportunity to ask questions and or make suggestions regarding Verizon's operations. I took advantage of this opportunity to discuss one of my pet peeves—the multiple copies of financial reports I receive each year from numerous public companies such as Verizon. Anyone with more than one brokerage account or with stock registered in more than one name is probably a recipient of these wasteful mailings. While those in the investment business are likely to be more aware of this problem, due to the proliferation of material sent to clients, I suspect many people are affected to some degree. The distribution of duplicate mailings wastes untold ink and paper and increases costs without producing any corresponding benefit. Verizon acknowledged the problem and promised to study how they could reduce duplicate mailings and still meet their legal requirements. The presentation ended with some suggestions about what each of us could do to reduce waste and save natural resources.

Collaborations at Work

The Sustainable Business Network teams with other organizations to co-sponsor workshops and conferences that provide mentoring and educational opportunities for its members. One such partnership is with the SVN's Social Venture Institute (SVI), which, since 1996, has provided a confidential forum for business leaders to discuss their challenges and obtain on-the-spot advice and assistance from appropriate experts. Attendees have the opportunity to participate in case study analyses, small group discussions led by knowledgeable panelists and a variety of plenary sessions. Successful, socially responsible business leaders provide professional advice and practical counsel and many long-term mentoring relationships and fruitful partnerships have been formed.[15]

SBN also sponsors an annual conference for local business people to learn ways of strengthening their enterprises. Their first one-day conference was held in conjunction with a multi-day conference with a "green building" theme. SBN's co-sponsor was the Delaware Valley Green Building Council. The aim of "green building" is to follow sustainable design practices so that a project can indefinitely support the construction, operation and renovation of environmentally sound buildings. Construction conforming to the Leadership in Energy and Environmental Design (LEED) rating system, developed by the U.S. Green Building Council, typically reduces operating costs, improves the indoor atmosphere and reduces the burden on the surrounding environment. A variety of workshops, covering everything from local sources of capital to sustainable, non-toxic cleaning and maintenance was presented. The exhibit hall showcased a wide variety of products and services. Lunch was prepared from local farm products and served during a fashion show of clothing by local designers. Judging by the larger than expected attendance, the extent of the networking and the feedback from a variety of people the conference was quite successful.

Impossible Dream?

BALLE's vision of a global economy composed of self-sufficient local communities networked with other sustainably developed communities may seem far-fetched to some. Some degree of skepticism is understandable; attaining this goal may require investors to accept a lower than average rate of return and consumers to pay a premium price for locally produced goods and services. Immense transnational corporations wielding enormous power both internationally and locally dominate the economy. Economies of scale make it possible for these companies to keep prices low and provide competitive returns to investors. But, with notable exceptions, these businesses tend to focus on short-term returns and evidence minimal concern for the environment or future generations.

It should be remembered, however, that most people were skeptical, if not derisive, when the idea of socially responsible business practices was first introduced and when the first socially responsible mutual funds were launched. In fact, the overwhelming assumption with respect to socially responsible investing was that such an approach would necessarily result in lower investment returns. With over a decade of data, an increasingly strong case can be made that companies acting in a socially responsible manner outperform their peers. Although neither SRB nor SRI thinking dominates the business scene, both have gained loyal advocates around the world; special interest organizations, central governments and the United Nations have all strongly encouraged these movements. What began as hesitant acquiescence has gradually become genuine commitment to improve socially responsible practices that enhance the reputation and productivity of most organizations. While there is solid evidence that investors are willing to put social consciences ahead of financial returns, how many are willing to make such sacrifices—and to what degree—is yet to be determined.

Many consumers already place their principles ahead of their pocketbooks and purchase products and services from businesses following socially responsible business practices. They are willing to pay premium prices for recycled material, hybrid powered cars, organic food, water and energy saving appliances, nonpolluting hydroelectric, wind and solar powered energy, non-insured alternative health practitioners, etc. In Pennsylvania, for example, tens of thousands of utility customers have switched to more costly nonpolluting "green energy" which saves 1,500 pounds of carbon dioxide per customer. According to a retired Pittsburgh pediatrician who switched to less polluting, renewable sources of electric energy, "It is a statement. It's something I feel strongly about." Even though more expensive than fossil fuel, wind powered energy is produced in more than half of the states across America, and generates enough energy to serve millions of households.[16]

Lakshman Krishnamurthi, Chairman of the marketing department at Northwestern University's Kellogg School of Management supports the proposition that premium prices are not necessarily an impediment to the sale of most goods and services. His observations confirm that customers are willing to pay more for quality. "Whether that quality is real or perceived is not relevant," according to professor Krishnamurthi. If a difference between your product and the competition is established, a psychological advantage is created. Echoing this stance is Gary Williams, CEO of Miller-Williams, which specializes in customer opinion measurement.

According to Miller, value and low cost are not synonymous.[17] Thus both theory and practice lend credence to BALLE's expectation that members of a local community will pay premium prices to secure a sustainable environment and a higher quality of life.

This is not to deny that many products and services can be produced or distributed more efficiently by nationally or internationally positioned companies. At a minimum, size and scale do matter when it comes to manufacturing and distributing large, complex pieces of technology that require extensive research and development budgets and that are sold internationally. Nonetheless, a growing number of people see the need for both vibrant local businesses and strong, socially responsible transnational corporations. Creating an environment where both approaches—investing locally to sustain globally and trading globally to prosper locally—can compete *and* cooperate serves the interests of all of *US*. In fact, healthy competition for the loyalty of investors and consumers encourages all businesses to re-examine the way their goods and services are offered. Ideally this will lead to the production of more goods and services that offer a healthy balance between quantity and quality.

This chapter has looked at innovative strategies communities have adopted to cope with the challenges of doing business in a global economy. The degree to which these approaches will prove successful is open to debate; the need for strategies centered on values that reflect an *US* mentality is indisputable.

Conclusion—The Audience is *US*

We conclude the book by asking an off-the-wall question. What do people fear most: deep water, snakes, heights, death? The answer—according to many surveys—is none of the above. What people fear most is speaking before an audience!

An oft-suggested antidote for this common phobia is to visualize the audience naked. Besides introducing a humorous and, therefore, relaxing image, this technique makes the audience appear exposed and vulnerable and less threatening to the speaker.

Participating in today's global marketplace—as a consumer, investor, businessperson or community member—can be as intimidating as speaking before a large group of people. Too many products cause harm, too many transactions are structured to be win/lose and scores of egomaniacs and self-serving authority figures care only about making a quick buck. The remedy is to raise consciousness so we recognize our interconnectedness and align our self-interest with the common good. Previous chapters have documented this age-old truth—values that emphasize inclusion and connection must be made a central part of our lives. We have seen concrete examples of how Visy and UPS, two large profitable MNCs, have benefited from making soul values an integral part of their operations. By producing environmentally sustainable products Visy has increased energy, resource and material efficiencies. UPS managers are more flexible and empathetic after attending the company's Community Intern Program. Supervisors with tolerant attitudes engender a more motivated and productive workforce with lower turnover. In a similar vein, The Djuma Game Reserve and White Dog Café's devoted customer base is directly related to their generous community involvement that, in turn, leads to an enhanced sense of fulfillment and self-worth for the principals of both establishments. More customers, greater loyalty, increased productivity—soul values are good for business. Changes that initially seem onerous—choosing to eliminate *ME* and *THEM* behavior—are often less arduous and far more rewarding than we imagine. As soul values become widespread and habitual, we will understand that the audience is *US* and we will be able to enter the global economy naked, fearless and free to pursue a truly conscious globalism.

Notes

[1] "Under Workers' Control," *The Economist*, 9 November 2002, 40.
[2] Lisa Garrigues, "Starting Over," *Yes! a Journal of Positive Futures*, Fall 2002, 23.
[3] Ibid.
[4] Ibid., 22.
[5] Trudy Rubin, "Worldview: Bold Measures in Brazil Give Poor a New Chance," *The Philadelphia Inquirer*, 25 April 2003, A19.
[6] Ibid.
[7] Kerry A. Dolan, "A New Kind of Entitlement," *Forbes*, 23 December 2002, 320.
[8] Josh Harkinson, "Profits of Place," *Orion*, January/February 2004, 60.
[9] "The Giving Tree," *The Philadelphia Inquirer*, 14 April 2003, A14.
[10] "New Study Shows Tree Deficit in the Philadelphia Area," *American Forests*, http://www.americanforest.org/news/print.php?id=108:16 April 2003.
[11] David C. Korten, "How Would We Live?" *Yes! a Journal of Positive Futures*, Fall 2002, 15.
[12] Ibid., 7–8.
[13] Harkinson, "Profits of Place," 62.
[14] Brochure, Greater Philadelphia Sustainable Business Network (Philadelphia, PA: 2002).
[15] Brochure, *Social Venture Institute* (Philadelphia, PA: 2002).
[16] Akweli Parker, "'Green' Power, Premium Price," *The Philadelphia Inquirer*, 10 April 2003, C1.
[17] Patrick Seitz, "Why Some Companies Can Levy Premium Prices and Others Not," *Investor's Business Daily*, 15 April 2003, A1.

References

Publications

Beresford, Dennis R., Nicholas deB. Katzenbach and C.B. Rogers. "Report of Investigation by the Special Investigative Committee of the Board of Directors of WorldCom, Inc.," Counsel: Wilmer, Cutler & Pickering; Accounting Advisors: PricewaterhouseCoopers LLP, 31 March 2003.

Breton, Denise and Christopher Largent. *The Paradigm Conspiracy: How Our Systems of Government, Church, School and Culture Violate Our Human Potential.* Center City, MN: Hazelden, 1996.

Breton, Denise and Christopher Largent. *The Soul of Economies: Spiritual Evolution Goes to the Marketplace.* Wilmington, DE: Idea House Publishing Company, 1991.

Cock, Jacklyn and Alison Bernstein. *Melting Pots & Rainbow Nations: Conversations About Difference in the United States and South Africa.* Urbana, IL: University of Illinois Press, 2002.

de Bruyn, Pippa. *Frommer's South Africa.* 2nd ed. New York: Hungry Minds, Inc., 2001.

DeRosa, David F. *In Defense of Free Capital Markets: The Case Against a New International Financial Architecture.* Princeton, NJ: Bloomberg Press, 2001.

Dossey, Larry. *Healing Words: The Power of Prayer and the Practice of Medicine*. San Francisco: HarperSanFrancisco, 1993.

Eland, Ivan. "The Empire Strikes Out: The 'New Imperialism' and its Fatal Flaws." *Cato Institute Policy Analysis*, 459 (26 November 2002).

Farrell, Larry C. *The Entrepreneurial Age: Awakening the Spirit of Enterprise in People, Companies, and Countries*. New York: Allworth Press, an imprint of Allworth Communications, 2001.

Friedman, Milton. *Capitalism and Freedom*. With the assistance of Rose D. Friedman. Phoenix Edition. Chicago: The University of Chicago Press, 1962.

Friedman, Thomas L. *The Lexus and the Olive Tree*. New York: Anchor Books, a division of Random House, Inc., 2000.

Gates, Jeffrey R. *The Ownership Solution: Toward a Shared Capitalism for the Twenty-first Century*. Reading, MA: Addison-Wesley, 1998.

Gwartney, James and Robert Lawson. *Economic Freedom of the World: 2002 Annual Report*. Vancouver, BC: The Fraser Institute, 2002.

Koh, Gillian and Ooi Giok Ling, ed. *State-Society Relations in Singapore*. Singapore: Oxford University Press, 2000.

Lay, Kenneth L., Jeffrey K. Skilling and Joseph W. Sutton. "To Our Shareholders." *Enron Annual Report*. 1999.

Loehr, Jim and Tony Schwartz. *The Power of Full Engagement*. New York: Free Press, a division of Simon & Schuster, Inc., 2003.

Malkiel, Burton G. "Socially Responsible Investing." *Classics II: Another Investor's Anthology*. Charles D. Ellis, ed. with James R. Vertin. Homewood, IL: Business One Irwin, 1991.

Max-Neef, Manfred. "Development and Human Needs." *Real-Life Economics: Understanding Wealth Creation*. Paul Ekins and Manfred Max-Neef, ed. London: Routledge, 1997.

McDonough, William and Michael Braungart. *Cradle to Cradle: Remaking the Way We Make Things*. New York: North Point Press, a division of Farrar, Straus and Giroux, 2002.

Morris, Kenneth M. *User's Guide to the Information Age*. New York: Lightbulb Press, Inc., 1999.

National Commission on Terrorist Attacks Upon the United States. *The 9/11 Commission Report*. New York: W. W. Norton & Company, 2004.

O'Driscoll, Gerald P. Jr., Kim R. Holmes and Mary A. O'Grady. *2002 Index of Economic Freedom*. The Heritage Foundation and the Wall Street Journal, 2002.

Powers, William C., Raymond S. Thoubh and Herbert S. Winokur Jr. "Report of Investigation by the Special Investigative Committee of the Board of Directors of Enron Corporation," Counsel: Wilmer, Cutler & Pickering. 1 February 2002.

Romero, Luis Alberto. *A History of Argentina in the Twentieth Century*. James B. Brennan, trans. University Park, PA: The Pennsylvania State University Press, 2002.

Samuelson, Paul A. *Economics: An Introductory Analysis*. 6th ed. New York: McGraw-Hill Book Company, 1964.

Schwerin, David A. *Conscious Capitalism: Principles for Prosperity*. Boston: Butterworth-Heinemann, 1998.

Singapore's Enterprise Ecosystem – Yearbook 2001/02. Singapore: Singapore Economic Development Board, September 2002.

Smith, Adam. *An Inquiry Into the Nature and Causes of the Wealth of Nations*. Edited with and introduction and commentary by Kathryn Sutherland. Oxford: Oxford University Press, 1993.

Thesenga, Susan. *The Undefended Self*. Charlottesville, VA: Pathwork Press, 2001.

Weiss, Joseph W. *Business Ethics: A Stakeholder and Issues Management Approach*. 2nd ed. Fort Worth, TX: The Dryden Press – Harcourt Brace College Publishers, 1998.

Wilson, Ian. *The New Rules of Corporate Conduct: Rewriting the Social Charter*. Westport, CT: Quorum Books, an Imprint of Greenwood Publishing Group, Inc., 2000.

Woodward, Bob. *The Agenda: Inside the Clinton White House*. New York: Simon & Schuster, 1994.

Web Sites

BALLE	*www.livingeconomies.org*
BigPictureSmallWorld	*www.bigpicturesmallworld.com*
Center for Global Development	*www.cgdev.org*
Conscious Globalism	*www.consciousthinking.com*
Djuma Game Reserve	*www.djuma.com*
The Earth Charter Initiative	*www.earthcharter.org*
European Baha'i Business Forum	*www.ebbf.org*
Global Education Motivators	*www.gem-ngo.org*
The Natural Step	*www.naturalstep.org*
Pathwork International	*www.pathwork.org*
Redefining Progress	*www.rprogress.org*
Seeds of Peace	*www.seedsofpeace.org*
White Dog Café Foundation	*www.whitedogcafefoundation.org*
A World Connected	*www.aworldconnected.org*

Index

About the Author

David A. Schwerin is the author of *Conscious Capitalism: Principles for Prosperity* published by Butterworth-Heinemann in 1998. His book has been translated into Portuguese and Chinese and is in its second printing in China. He has over thirty years of business experience, beginning as a financial analyst and senior investment officer with a large bank and then founding D J Investment Advisors, Inc., serving as its president since 1976. David has taught economics on the college level and has given expert witness testimony on financial matters, his articles have been published worldwide and he has often been quoted in the press.

David received his undergraduate degree in Business, a MBA in Finance and a Ph.D. in Religious Studies. He was awarded membership in Beta Gamma Sigma, national business honor society and is a member of the Financial Analysts Federation and The Sustainable Business Network. He serves on the board of directors of a number of non-profit organizations and is Chairman of the Pathwork Press.

David has given lectures, presentations and radio and TV interviews throughout the U.S. In 2001 and 2002 he gave over a dozen lectures on a variety of business topics to political leaders, business executives and academic audiences in eight cities in China.